African Energy
Issues in Planning and Practice

African Energy Policy Research Network
(AFREPREN)

Zed Books Ltd
London and New Jersey

African Energy Policies: Issues in Planning and Practice
as first published by Zed Books Ltd, 57 Caledonian Road
London N1 9BU, UK, and 171 First Avenue,
Atlantic Highlands, New Jersey 07716, in 1990.

Copyright © African Energy Research Policy Network
(AFREPREN), 1990.

Cover designed by Sophie Buchet.
Typeset by Opus 43, Broughton-in-Furness.
Printed and bound in the United Kingdom
by Biddles Ltd, Guildford and King's Lynn.

All rights reserved.

British Library Cataloguing in Publication data

African Energy policies: issues in planning and practice.
1. Africa. Energy resources
I. African Energy Policy Research Network
333.79096

ISBN 0-86232-912-4
ISBN 0-86232-913-2 pbk

Contents

	Acknowledgements	vii
	Abbreviations	ix
	Preface	xi
	A Note on AFREPREN A. Datta	xviii
1.	**Introduction** M.R. Bhagavan, D. Brooks, Haile Lul Tebicke and S. Karekezi	1
2.	**Renewable Energy Technologies**	13
2.1	S.A. Bachou: *New approaches to the development and utilisation of renewable energy resources in Uganda*	15
2.2	S. Karekezi: *Review of mature renewable energy technologies in sub-Saharan Africa*	20
2.3	J. Katihabwa: *Solar hot water for household and institutional use in Bujumbura, Burundi*	25
2.4	D. Mbewe: *Effectiveness of research and policy on rural energy technology and applications*	30
3.	**Bio-energy**	35
3.1	I.A.R. Elgizouli: *Rural–urban household energy use and inter-relation in the central region of the Sudan*	37
3.2	P. Karenzi: *Rural and poor urban energy situation In Rwanda*	42
3.3	D.L. Kgathi: *A critical review of fuelwood surveys in Botswana*	48
4.	**Electricity**	55
4.1	Haile Lul Tebicke and Hailu Gebre Mariam: *A case study of small hydro and grid extension for rural electrification alternatives and complementarities*	57
4.2	L.M. Khalema: *Energy demand and consumption patterns of Maseru peri-urban areas, with particular reference to low-income locations*	64
4.3	M. L. Luhanga (in collaboration with B.E. Luhanga): *Opportunities and prospects for energy conservation in the Tanzania Electric Supply Company Limited*	69
4.4	A. Mbewe: *Opportunities and prospects for energy conservation in an electrical utility: a Zambian case*	77
4.5	I. Ntirizoshira: *Hydro-electricity and peat as alternatives to fuel oil in the industrial sector in Burundi*	81

5. Coal and Gasification — 87
5.1 I. Ali Ahmed: *Options for power generation in Somalia* — 89
5.2 R.S. Maya (in collaboration with N.N. Wekwete): *Issues and prospects for coal utilisation in Zimbabwe's rural households* — 94
5.3 M.P. Modisi: *Coal resources availability in Botswana: an assessment of present and future demand* — 99
5.4 A.N. Ng'andu (in collaboration with A.M. Mwanza): *The influence of comparative price in the substitution of coal for woodfuel and charcoal: the Zambian case* — 106

6. Oil and Natural Gas — 111
6.1 J. Baguant (in collaboration with R.P. Beeharry and J. Manrakhan): *Exploring the possibility of using low grade ethanol as a kerosene substitute for cooking* — 113
6.2 M.J. Mwandosya: *Technical skill acquisition in the Tanzanian oil sector* — 118

7. Institutions and Planning — 125
7.1 L. Mohapeloa and M. Lebesa: *The effectiveness of foreign technical assistance in manpower development in Lesotho's energy projects* — 127
7.2 J. Morgan: *Energy models as policy tools* — 132
7.3 P.M. Nyoike and B.A. Okech: *Rationality of Kenyan energy demand management* — 138
7.4 Mengistu Teferra: *The applicability of the 'Bangladesh Model' for energy demand forecast in Ethiopia* — 143

Notes on contributors — 149
Photograph of AFREPREN conference participants — 152
Index — 153

Acknowledgements

A large number of individuals and institutions, both official and private, have assisted the authors in many ways. They are too numerous to be mentioned here by name. The authors gratefully acknowledge this invaluable help and extend their sincere thanks.

The staff of the National Institute of Development Research and Documentation (NIR) of the University of Botswana deserve warm thanks for the administrative support given to the authors during the course of their research.

Generous financial and professional support by the Canadian International Development Research Centre (IDRC) and the Swedish Agency for Research Cooperation with Developing Countries (SAREC) is gratefully acknowledged. Thanks are also due to SAREC for financing the publication of this volume.

Abbreviations

ADNOC	Abu Dhabi National Oil Corporation
AFREPREN	African Energy Policy Research Network
AFVP	French Association of Volunteers for Progress
BRET	Botswana Renewable Technology Project
BUNEP	National Bureau of Study Projects (Rwanda)
cal	calorie/s
CEAER	Energy Research and Application Centre of the National University of Rwanda
CESEN	Italian Energy Consultants (contracted by the Ethiopian Ministry of Mines and Energy)
cm	centimetre(s)
CSC	Commonwealth Science Council
COTEBU	Burundi Textile Company
ECUP	Expanded Coal Utilisation Project (Botswana)
EELPA	Ethiopian Electric Authority
ENEE	National Electric Utility (Somalia)
ENI	Italian National Petroleum Corporation
EPFL	Ecole Polytechnique Fédérale de Lausanne
ERL	Energy Resources Ltd
ESAC	Eastern and Southern African Countries
ESCOM	Electricity Supply Commission of South Africa
ESMAP	Energy Sector Management Assistance Programme
FAO	Food and Agriculture Organisation
FBu	Burundi Francs
GDP	Gross Domestic Product
gj	gigajoule(s)
GOL	Government of Lesotho
gwh	gigawatt hour(s)
ha	hectares
hz	hertz
IDRC	International Development Research Centre (Canada)
ITDG	Intermediate Technology Development Group
JEEP	Joint Energy and Environment Projects
K	Kwacha (Zambian currency)
kcal	kilocalorie(s)
KCJ	Kenya Ceramic Jiko (cooking stove project)
kg	kilogram(s)
kj	kilojoule(s)
km	kilometre(s)
kv	kilovolt(s)
kva	kilovolt-ampere(s)
kw	kilowatt(s)
kwh	kilowatt hour(s)
LPG	liquid petroleum gas

M	Maloti (Lesotho currency)
m	metre(s)
mhz	megahertz
mj	megajoule(s)
mm	millimetre(s)
mt	metric tonne(s)
mw	megawatt(s)
mwh	megawatt hour(s)
NDP	Norwegian Petroleum Directorate
NGO	non-governmental organisation
NIOC	National Iranian Oil Corporation
NIR	National Institute of Development Research and Documentation (Botswana)
NORAD	Norwegian Agency for Development Cooperation
ODA	Official Development Assistance
ONCCP	Central Planning Office (Ethiopia)
ONGC	Oil and Natural Gas Corporation of India
P	Pula (Botswana currency)
PSA	Petroleum Sharing Agreement
R(s)	Rupees (Mauritian currency)
RES	Reference Energy System
RET	Renewable Energy Technology
ROM	run-of-mine (coal)
SADCC	Southern African Development Coordination Conference
SAREC	Swedish Agency for Research Cooperation with Developing Countries
SHIPINDIA	Shipping Corporation of India
SNV	Netherlands Voluntary Service
STATOIL	State Oil Corporation of Norway
TAG	Technical Assistance Group
TANESCO	Tanzania Electric Supply Company Ltd
TIPER	Tanzanian and Italian Petroleum Refinery Company
Toe	tonne of oil equivalent
TPDC	Tanzanian Petroleum Development Corporation
TShs	Tanzanian Shillings
UNCTAD	United Nations Conference on Trade and Development
UNDP	United Nations Development Programme
UNEDO	Uganda National Energy Development Organisation
USAID	United States Agency for International Development
w	watt(s)
WB	World Bank
YWCA	Young Women's Christian Association
ZESCO	Zambia Electricity Supply Corporation Ltd

Preface:
The Creation of the African Energy Policy Research Network (AFREPREN)

M.R. Bhagavan

The need for the network

Over the last two decades, the countries of sub-Saharan Africa have been subjected to several extremely grave crises, caused by factors both internal and external, both man-made and natural. Among these are the crises in both the modern and traditional energy sectors. Since energy cuts across the whole of the economy, its crisis has caused severe disruptions in virtually every section of society. Prime indicators of the energy crisis are the drastic reduction in the import of crude and refined petroleum products; deterioration in the electricity generating and distributing equipment due to cuts in the imports of spare parts, new equipment, and repair and maintenance know-how; and soil erosion or desertification in the savannahs and dry forests.

By the very nature of their responsibilities and tasks, African policy-makers have had to resort to short-term crisis-management measures. While they are aware in a general sense that research on a broad front in the technical, economic and social fields may make a significant contribution to the formulation and implementation of sound and practical policies, they may still need to be fully convinced that research is essential for solving problems in the medium and long term. And on the other side of the coin, researchers inside and outside Africa may not have appreciated fully the indispensability of close contact with policy-makers for the choice of research topics that would be highly relevant and significant for overcoming the problems posed by the crisis.

It would therefore be valuable to bring together researchers and policy-makers in a network so as to sensitise each other on their respective problems, perspectives and priorities. Since energy is of immediate practical interest, the approach to the energy establishment has to be different from the conventional one of 'academic research'. The themes and topics that would interest the energy establishment depend on whom one is talking to. Non-establishment figures — a description that would fit most researchers today — have very limited influence at present.

But research ideology has its limits: research cannot be expected to provide practical solutions to every problem that crops up. Further, policy-makers have to be made aware that it may not be possible to handle immediate problems requiring short-term solutions without simultaneous attention to long-term perspectives and solutions. It may well be that solutions to major problems can come from 'fringe' research. New types of thinking have to be opened up and one has to find out what topics and approaches would capture the attention of the policy-makers.

The countries of sub-Saharan Africa display several common features which are integral to the origin and evolution of the crisis: a fragile economic, social and higher-educational infrastructure; shortcomings in the quantity, quality and diversity of skilled people; extreme dependence on a few export crops and minerals for earning hard convertible currencies, etc. They have similar ecological zones, natural resources, population distribution and agricultural practices. Given these similarities, certain energy research areas of relevance to energy policy-making and energy planning may be tackled best on a sub-regional basis in the most resource-effective way, while other areas will necessarily be country-specific. A network would be ideal for identifying, classifying and discussing research problems specific to sub-regions, and how best to organise work on them.

There is some research going on in the region, and some research skills have been created. But this research work is mainly on the 'hardware' aspect of Renewable Energy Technologies (RETs). Only rarely does current research help policy-makers in their work. The focus on economic, social and cultural aspects is weak. There are substantial gaps in knowledge that would enable policy-makers to intervene in a positive and constructive way.

There is now a growing awareness that the energy crisis is not amenable to purely technical (i.e., hardware) solutions, nor to solutions which are entirely supply-oriented. Economic, social and cultural factors play an equally decisive role in an approach that includes need, demand and end-use orientation. The network would deliberate on the relative balances of these various dimensions and factors as they apply to specific problem areas, and wherever possible identify the corresponding leading dimensions.

Policy-makers are understandably looking for quick ways of obtaining research results that they can use in crisis management. This more often than not means, firstly, a recourse to expatriate researchers based in the industrially and technologically developed countries, and, secondly, funding by foreign agencies to pay for the services of the expatriate researchers. While this is a perfectly reasonable and legitimate method to adopt in the short term, it is untenable in the medium and long term. The solutions to local, national and sub-regional problems cannot be sustained unless national research capacity is built up. Further, it is by no means certain that foreign researchers would be able to produce research results which can be applied successfully to problems requiring an intimate non-technical understanding of the local environment. It is therefore a matter of urgent priority that African policy-makers and researchers should deliberate together on how best to allocate the limited resources available to them. They must decide when to obtain quick research results and when to build up national and sub-regional research capacity in terms of research personnel, infrastructure and institutions. One does not, of course, exclude the other.

While it is important *firstly* to pursue alternative institutional structures for getting research done, and *secondly* to promote research *about* institutions, it would be wise to build on, and support, existing structures and institutions.

The number of energy researchers in Africa is very small at present. To attract more researchers into the energy area and to broaden its base, one has to involve and support researchers from adjacent, relevant areas which are not strictly 'energy topics' in the narrow sense: this is particularly so for the non-technological (i.e. economic, social and cultural) dimensions.

In deciding 'what to do research on' and 'how to do research', it is as important to be guided by research practitioners and existing research structures and institutions as by the views of the policy-makers and the establishment.

It is important to create 'demand' for research among policy-makers, and to make them aware of the existence of ongoing research in their countries.

The process of setting up the network

In May 1987 a small preparatory meeting in Gaborone, Botswana was hosted by the National Institute of Development Research and Documentation (NIR) of the University of Botswana, with support from the Canadian International Development Research Centre (IDRC) and the Swedish Agency for Research Cooperation with Developing Countries (SAREC). Six African researchers and policy-makers of high standing took part. The meeting identified a number of topics of central importance for energy policy and energy planning research in Africa in the following six sectors: (1) RETs, (2) bio-energy, (3) electricity, (4) oil and natural gas, (5) coal and gasification and (6) institutions and planning. It was decided to convene a two-week workshop in November—December 1987 in Gaborone on 'Energy Policy and Energy Planning Research in East Africa and Southern Africa'.

The workshop was organised by NIR, with assistance from IDRC and SAREC. The 30 African researchers and policy-makers who attended came from Botswana, Burundi, Ethiopia, Kenya, Lesotho, Mozambique, Rwanda, the Seychelles, Somalia, the Sudan, Swaziland, Tanzania, Uganda, Zambia and Zimbabwe. Eight resource persons of international repute from Canada, China, Ethiopia, Ghana, Sweden, the UK and the USA, chosen for their expertise in the six sectors mentioned above, also attended, and assisted the sector groups. The workshop discussed in considerable detail and depth the topics put forward by the May 1987 preparatory meeting (see below), and decided to undertake 26 short research studies as the next stage in setting up the network.

Twenty-two of the planned 26 studies were completed during 1988, and presented at a second workshop held by NIR in Gaborone in March 1989. Summarised versions of these are presented in Parts 2 to 7 of this volume. The research studies, as well as the March 1989 workshop, were funded by IDRC and SAREC.

The 30 African energy researchers and energy policy-makers attending the March 1989 workshop decided to launch the African Energy Policy

Research Network (AFREPREN) with six major research programmes which are listed below. The AFREPREN Programme for the 1989–91 period will be funded by SAREC.

AFREPREN's six research programmes for 1989–91, with participating researchers and policy-makers

Title	Participant	Country
1. Key factors for the dissemination of Rural Energy Technologies and bio-energy interventions	S.A. Bachou I.A. Elgizouli S. Karekezi J. Katihabwa D. Mbewe F. Neto M. Theko	Uganda Sudan Kenya Burundi Zambia Angola Lesotho
2. Use of biomass energy balance to determine the woodfuel problem	P.C. Karenzi D.L. Kgathi	Rwanda Botswana
3. Rural electrification: main issues in decentralisation and pricing of electricity generation and supply	I. Ali Ahmed Hailu G. Mariam L.M. Khalema M.L. Luhanga A. Mbewe I. Ntirizoshira B.R. Ramasedi	Somalia Ethiopia Lesotho Tanzania Zambia Burundi Botswana
4. Substitution of coal for other fuels in household and institutional applications: a critical analysis of the technological and socio-economic prerequisites, and environmental impacts	J.S.B. Dipaha R.S. Maya A.N. Ng'andu	Botswana Zimbabwe Zambia
5. Efficient use of petroleum products: opportunities and constraints in the household, transport and electricity generation sectors	J. Baguant Mengistu Teferra M. Mwandosya	Mauritius Ethiopia Tanzania
6. Institutions and planning appropriate to energy demand management	L. Mohapeloa J. Morgan F.O. Motlhatlhedi P.M. Nyoike B.A. Okech	Lesotho Seychelles Botswana Kenya Kenya

Preface xiii

Energy issues discussed at AFREPREN's planning meeting in May 1987 in Gaborone, Botswana

RETs

Review the experiences of RET dissemination.

Methodologies and strategies for effective dissemination of RETs based on experiences from East African, Southern African and other regions.

Dissemination often boils down to the question of finances: how expensive it is for rural buyers; subsidies, loans and credits by public sector; commercialisation by private sector.

Bio-energy

Review of existing studies to identify gaps and weaknesses in supply, demand and end-use in bio-energy.

Methodologies of research and surveys of end-use consumption to establish commonality of parameters and approaches.

Policy implications of urban energy supply alternatives to meet shortfalls.

New methodologies research geared to policy-makers' needs.

Policies for making self-sustained bio-energy harvesting regimes economically and socially acceptable, paying attention in particular to rules and regulations on harvesting.

Reviews of sustainable energy inputs into increasing productivity of small farms, with particular attention to import and foreign exchange components, with a view to developing appropriate policies.

Electricity

Capacity and performance: where money losses occur, how and why they occur.

Electricity generation and distribution performance: repair and maintenance, spare parts advance planning, ageing machinery. The key question of management efficiency. Summary of available studies to identify new research that will interest policy-makers. Studies of these problems by the top executives of electricity utilities would be very valuable.

Deferred costs and other penalties of large generating stations in a climate of low-capacity utilisation.

Projected future effective demand for capacity to absorb electricity by 'decentralised' users in small towns, large villages, etc. Foreign exchange generation through electricity-consumption-intensive enterprises, especially terms of external trade affecting electricity pricing — e.g., consumer goods for export, processed minerals for export, etc.

Studies on relative prices, tariffs and subsidies along the same lines as in oil.

Coal and gasification

Policy-related research studies on pollution and other environmental aspects of the mining and use of coal.

Role of institutional arrangements for coal gasification and production of synthetic liquid hydrocarbons.

Oil and natural gas

The oil substitution question to be addressed through demand pattern analysis and demand management, taking conservation into account.

How policy-makers dealt with the crises: what can we learn about crisis management that could be useful for the future?

Policy and pricing: effect of devaluation on collapse of oil prices — who bears the cost?

How realistic are price mechanisms?

Viability and effectiveness of physical rationing and other physical supply constraints in oil on consumers.

Effect on vehicular transport sector of petroleum refinery distillate differential. This is to be dealt with under demand management. Similarly with electrification and coal. Switching effects between railways and roads.

Fuel substitution as a general topic.

Foreign trade: alternative supply sources of oil, competitive markets, barter: information and analysis of these. Terms of trade of commodities which are oil-based, and oil-intensive.

The horizons for building local capacity in oil exploration, etc.: regional vs national capacity — effective use of these. Sub-topics to be covered: partnership with whom; bottlenecks in implementation; what to do with capacity having once built it?

Policy analysis of economics of exploration and exploitation of oil. See UNCTAD studies on structure and legal aspects of oil exploration as a preliminary before launching studies in this area.

Institutions

Essential concept of handling policy, implemented policy, how to make policy operational. The middle-level policy implementers need to understand the policy-makers' intent. Kinds of management needed in implementing policy.

Process of producing policy alternatives for decision-makers.

Vested interests: constraints on policy-makers and policy-implementers. Modalities and mechanisms of policy initiatives and policy changes as they work their way through the government structures.

Target groups for the participants in the research workshops: heads of technical departments in ministries and senior counterpart researchers outside government, heads of public authorities. Very important to involve heads of finance departments.

Links between policy-makers and researchers very important as a way of overcoming lack of skills in government for doing in-depth research.

Concept of efficiency in general at an aggregate level. Dimensions of management and organisation. Efficiency from a supply, demand and end-use perspective to be taken up at the sectoral levels.

Planning

Planning concerns both national possibilities and constraints and their interface with international constraints.

Energy planning to be integrated within energy sectors and between energy sectors, and between energy and other sectors.

Integrated energy planning is necessary and important for small countries with resource constraints. Policy-makers would be interested in this idea.

Analysis of planning, both integrated and otherwise, in some countries of the East African and Southern African regions.

Tools needed for co-ordination between different institutions: how to devise the means to integrate (institutional aspects of this very important).

Analysis of World Bank's 'changed' attitudes to policies and institutions in developing countries; in particular World Bank's recent 'positive' support for local capacity building and research, and consultancy done by local people.

Collection of primary data (raw data, field data) on energy sources.

Tools and methods of planning.

Resource and technology assessment: information accessibility to assessment making, local capacity for technical and resource assessment.

A Note on the Co-ordination and Administration of AFREPREN

A. Datta

The process by which AFREPREN was set up has been described in the Preface. We will therefore confine ourselves here to highlighting the main features involved in co-ordinating and administering the network, which encompasses firstly the relations between researchers, policy-makers, the co-ordinating agency and the sponsors; secondly, the co-ordinating agency's role; and thirdly, the dissemination and use of the network's output.

The University of Botswana was called upon to co-ordinate and administer the network, a task which was entrusted by the university to its National Institute of Development Research and Documentation (NIR). The philosophy and basic direction of NIR, as well as its structure and functioning, have understandably shaped the quality and style of the co-ordination that the Institute has been able to provide.

The main objective of NIR, as set out by the University of Botswana Statutes of 1982, is to carry out research on issues relating to 'socio-economic, environmental and cultural development affecting Botswana'. Already four years prior to the enactment of the Statutes, NIR had created an environmental research unit. This unit, because of its early start and the support it has received, is the largest in the Institute in terms of its professional staff and scientific output.

The work of administering the activities of AFREPREN entails five main functions: (1) liaising with researchers, theme co-ordinators, resource persons and sponsors; (2) disbursements of funds to the researchers, and other financial activities integral to the running of the network; (3) organising periodic regional workshops; (4) preparation of technical and financial reports; and (5) reproducing and distributing the network's research output. As the administrative capacity of the Institute was quite stretched in servicing the Institute's ongoing work, it became necessary to appoint a part-time professional administrator to deal with the network.

Besides an administrator, the network clearly required the services of an energy professional who could deal with the technical aspects of co-ordinating the work in the six AFREPREN research programmes mentioned in the Preface. To fulfil this function, a Nairobi-based member of AFREPREN was appointed to act as a part-time network facilitator. He combines this role with his other roles in the network as a researcher and theme co-ordinator. While the division of co-ordination between Gaborone and Nairobi has its obvious problems, it has also manifest advantages for a network as widely spread as AFREPREN's.

Botswana enjoys certain advantages such as relatively smooth foreign exchange transactions entailed in disbursing research funds to various countries in the network, good air connections and telecommunications with East Africa and Southern Africa, and an ethos of relatively efficient administration. Further, the country has accumulated a certain amount of experience in conducting environmental research which is useful in the context of administering the network. Similarly, Nairobi has certain advantages, in particular its air connections and telecommunications, and an infrastructure created for the functioning of regional and international activities.

A challenge which NIR has had to face was the addition of its role as AFREPREN's administrator to its other roles within Botswana. The Institute's primary responsibility is to its mother organisation, the University of Botswana. Simultaneously, in its role as a *national* institute it has to fulfil certain expectations held by the governmental ministries and parastatals, the non-governmental organisations, and the general public. Furthermore, the Institute has its own research and consultancy work to look after. One consequence of taking on the administration of AFREPREN is that a sizeable portion of the time and energy of the Institute's staff and Director have to be spent on the network. Fortunately, NIR's commitment to promoting regional research, and to the strengthening of regional networks, is in keeping with the priorities of Botswana.

Researchers are proverbially individualistic, being accustomed to their own particular styles of functioning. But they have to operate within frameworks which are being progressively 'bureaucratised'. Within the confines of the same society, certain expectations and norms are taken for granted. But in the present case, with network participants hailing from diverse societies, cultures and traditions — stretching from the Sudan in the north to Lesotho in the south, from Angola on the Atlantic to the Seychelles in the Indian Ocean — the constraints are liable to be experienced as even more complex and compelling. If one adds to this the problems of the physical means of transportation and communication within the African continent, the allegiance to different cognitive specialisations, and the unpredictable chemistry of human relations, it would have been surprising if very delicate and sensitive issues had not cropped up. But happily such contingencies have been rare in the life of the network so far. Such challenges have called forth innovations in methods of co-ordination and administration by the Institute's staff, which is an asset to the region.

NIR's relationship with AFREPREN's sponsors SAREC and IDRC are close and warm. From the very beginning, when exploratory work was being undertaken to identify potential members of the network, the representatives of NIR, SAREC and IDRC were able to establish professional and personal rapport. The two sponsors have been generous with funds. They have also shared their professional expertise in the energy research area with the network.

It is useful to indicate the different levels at which the research process can be fruitfully co-ordinated. In elaborating the role of NIR as the co-ordinating agency we have so far dealt with official levels, i.e. with policy-makers working in government institutions and researchers in universities. However, there remain other important levels which need to be brought into the network, in particular the non-governmental organisations active in energy research in the region. Such a move will avoid duplication, facilitate a wider exchange of ideas and experiences, and provide resources for research to other relevant individuals and bodies. One can add yet another significant component into the network by establishing 'reference groups' of peers, as well as producers and consumers of energy, to advise each of the six theme groups now comprising AFREPREN. This will help, among other things, the integration of the findings of the research teams into policy-making and policy implementation on a much wider basis throughout the region. Contacts with networks dealing with subjects other than energy will also contribute to AFREPREN's learning of the networking process.

1 Introduction

1 Introduction

M.R. Bhagavan, D. Brooks, Haile Lul Tebicke and S. Karekezi

The twenty-two papers that appear in this volume are highly condensed versions of the much longer originals which were presented at AFREPREN's workshop in Gaborone in March 1989. Although brief, each of them sets out the main purpose of the study, the methodology used, the main findings arrived at and the policy conclusions reached. We sketch below the broad outlines of the issues raised by these studies and the recommendations they make.

Renewable Energy Technologies

Renewable Energy Technologies (RETs) have, in the eyes of many, failed to fulfil their promise. In the early 1970s, RETs were seen as a panacea for sub-Saharan Africa's deteriorating energy situation. Over the last fifteen years, significant financial resources were invested in RET projects. Today, RETs continue to face daunting problems. It is the solution of these problems that provides the primary rationale for the research studies on RETs presented in Part 2 of this publication. The research studies were undertaken by policy-makers and researchers from four countries of East, Central and Southern Africa, namely Zambia, Uganda, Burundi and Kenya.

D. Mbewe examines RET projects in Zambia with a special focus on the crucial link between policy-makers and researchers in the renewable energy sector. Using information from case studies that encompass a wide range of RETs (energy-efficient kilns, improved cooking stoves, biogas plants, wind-pumps, hay box cookers and solar water heaters), Mbewe identifies the key problems that face renewable energy projects in Zambia. The most important problems are:

- excessive reliance on external financial and technical assistance without checking on its relevance to the energy needs and priorities of the local population and without a clear understanding of the strings that are often tied to the offer of assistance;
- lack of adequate incentives for local RET researchers.

To tackle the above problems, Mbewe recommends increased contribution by host governments to RET projects in Zambia and the establishment of attractive financial incentives for local researchers in the form of consultancy fees and contracts.

In contrast to Mbewe's emphasis on institutional constraints on the development of RETs in Zambia, S. Bachou concentrates on the technical and economic obstacles that continue to slow the development of RETs in Uganda. His research study provides a panoramic view of the new and renewable energy resources in Uganda and discusses the key activities undertaken by governments and non-governmental organisations (NGOs) in the renewable energy sector. It also examines, in detail, the events that led to the creation of a new umbrella non-governmental agency (Uganda National Energy Development Organisation, UNEDO) whose primary mandate is to co-ordinate renewable energy activities undertaken by grassroots agencies and voluntary organisations in Uganda.

Continuing the same technical trend, J. Katihabwa discusses the theoretical and scientific rationale for the introduction of solar water heaters in Bujumbura, the capital of Burundi. Using meteorological data that date as far back as 1961, and a detailed assessment of classical solar collector theory, Katihabwa provides an articulate and concise theoretical and scientific basis for the initiation of a major solar water heater project in Bujumbura.

The RET section in this publication includes a generic research study carried out by S. Karekezi, a Kenya-based researcher. His study identifies the following key factors that are important prerequisites for successful dissemination of RETs in sub-Saharan Africa:
- base-line information on renewable energy resources;
- coherent national energy policy guidelines for the development of RETs;
- renewable energy research, together with technical and maintenance skills;
- wide-scale dissemination and commercialisation strategies.

Bio-energy

The three papers in the bio-energy section (Part 3) are on the fuelwood problems in Botswana, Rwanda and the Sudan. In each, scarcity of fuelwood — which in rural areas used to be gathered, and in urban areas bought at prices rapidly soaring to unaffordable levels — is being experienced by increasing numbers of households, in particular by the poor. Accordingly, in these countries as elsewhere in Africa, three main measures have been advocated and recently pursued, often with loans and grants from a variety of sources. Fuelwood plantations have been developed to enhance supplies; other household fuels have been introduced; and efficient cooking stoves have been disseminated to reduce fuelwood demand growth.

D. L. Kgathi, a researcher at the University of Botswana, argues that methodological flaws in seven studies (1983—1988) on the fuelwood problem in his country make the data gathered of doubtful value. He sees a need for comprehensive, rigorous study of the fuelwood problem that would reveal the severity of the scarcity, the social strata most affected by it, and the efficacy in 'real life situations' of the measures mentioned above. Such a study would provide a firm basis for an integrated strategy to overcome the fuelwood problem in Botswana.

Karenzi, of the National University of Rwanda, reports on the energy situation of the rural and urban poor in his country. He cites a 1983 report on Rwanda's energy sector which, on the basis of an estimated 2.8 million cubic metres annual excess of fuelwood off-take over natural and plantation regrowth in Rwanda, projected total depletion of reserves by 1985. Fortunately, this catastrophe did not occur, apparently because of the widespread rural practice of using tree and crop residues as household fuel, which had been overlooked in making the prediction. The National Energy Policy elaborated in 1983 had envisaged, among other things, large-scale pursuit of the three above-mentioned measures to counter the fuelwood problem. The most visible implementation of the policy so far was the planting of 19,000 hectares of trees in 1984. But also noteworthy is the widespread campaign, conducted through school curricula and as an integral part of all rural development projects, to bring home to people the possibilities of economising on household fuelwood and energy. Karenzi also sees a need for an in-depth study into the real needs of rural people for fuelwood and into its uses, and especially into the role of crop residues.

An analysis of the uses and inter-relations of energy in rural and urban households of the Central Region of the Sudan convinces I.A.R. Elgizouli of the National Energy Administration that millions of rural and urban people will face a fuelwood problem, because annual off-take rates are far in excess of regrowth. Use of crop and animal residues as fuel is increasing rapidly in the region, especially in Gezira province where wood is now very scarce. Market prices of woody biomass are soaring whereas production and supply costs remain low especially for charcoal, the preferred urban household fuel. The fuelwood and charcoal trade has become very lucrative and applies increasing pressure of deforestation as urbanisation is growing very rapidly in this region. Elgizouli considers a detailed resources assessment necessary to determine the actual situation, especially for wood, so that strategic plans may be drawn up for an effective combination of programmes to be pursued in afforestation, fuel switching and efficient cooking stove dissemination.

There can be no doubt that household fuelwood use is one among several factors in the disastrous decimation of forests and tree- and shrub-stands that is causing household fuel scarcity and environmental degradation in Africa. But what is its contribution to this catastrophic situation relative to other population-driven causes such as land-clearing, most often by the slash-and-burn method, to produce (with low-yielding, area-extensive agricultural techniques) ever more food for inexorably growing population numbers? Or the use of tree stems, branches, shrub-wood and even grasses, in rural and urban areas alike, for essential purposes such as construction of houses, shelters, fences, the making of furniture, implements, tools, utensils, woodcraft products, etc.? In these circumstances, when could the above-mentioned measures, applied extensively in 'real-life situations', be expected to stem and reverse fuelwood scarcity and ultimate biofuel famine for the rapidly increasing number of African households? How likely is attainment of sustainable patterns of bio-energy supply and efficient use by the growing populations inhabiting Africa's many fragile ecologies, and especially those prone to cyclic drought? Bio-energy policy and planning research must seek answers to these questions as well!

Electricity

Hailu Gebre Mariam and Haile Lul Tebicke investigated small-hydro plants as alternatives to either stand-alone diesel generators or grid extension for rural electrification in Ethiopia. Basing their analysis on a case study of a market town with 5,000 inhabitants and a hydro site some 25 km away, they found that a 600 kw hydro plant would entail higher capital costs than diesel costs and higher operating costs than grid extension, but would offer lower maintenance costs and foreign exchange requirements than either of the two conventional options. Thus, small hydro turned out to be the preferable option even though it was slightly higher in annualised investment cost than diesel. The authors also suggested that diesel created more opportunities for manufacturing components and developing technical capacity in Ethiopia, under a wide variety of circumstances.

Lucy M. Khalema investigated the potential demand for electricity in households located in the peri-urban areas of Maseru. Based on a survey of electrified and non-electrified households, and a review of technical information, the study sought to determine why electricity demand was so low, particularly in light of a government subsidy. The survey showed that most households were enthusiastic about the prospects of electrification but that a number of barriers related to the cost of connection and the cost of electricity suppressed demand from low- to middle-income residents. Ms Khalema concluded that there were a number of options open to Lesotho Electricity Corporation to stimulate demand in ways that would eventually become economically self-supporting.

Abel Mbewe and Matthew L. Luhanga, located respectively in Zambia and Tanzania, investigated the potential for electricity conservation in a national electrical utility. They showed that conservation within the utility offers a viable and effective way to increase deliverable capacity, which is particularly welcome in a time of both growing demand and capital shortage. Undertaking energy audits over all stages of production from primary inputs to plant sales, they defined the technical and economic potential for savings. They also developed a method to identify the theft of power. In the Zambian system, generation losses are now quite low (6.5 per cent) but technical and non-technical retail losses are high.

Isaie Ntirizoshira investigated hydro-electricity and peat as substitutes for fuel oil in Burundi's industrial sector. Because Burundi is land-locked, oil products are particularly expensive, and, according to a survey, the potential for substitution in industry amounts to 10 mw. However, cost analysis shows that, under current pricing schemes, even hydro-electricity is too expensive to be considered feasible. Peat, on the other hand, offers real opportunities for reducing oil use. It is widely available and low in cost, even after allowance for lower efficiency in combustion. A case study of one textile plant with a 2 mw demand indicated that annual costs could be cut by over 40 per cent, which yields a payback period of less than three years on the procurement and installation of new boilers.

Coal and gasification

I. Ali Ahmed compared the alternatives of supplying electricity in Somalia by use of imported oil, imported coal, or imported electricity. At present, Somalia has both a low level of demand (26 kwh per capita) and limited ability to generate (less than 70 mw). Almost all of the nation's electricity is produced in diesel generators and, except for the capital Mogadishu, supply is not reliable. Using four northern regions as a case study area, Ahmed prepared a load forecast and identified a need for an additional 20 mw of power. Turning to cost estimates for the three options, he found coal-fired steam turbines to be the cheapest, and he recommended that the government both improve the maintenance of existing stations and construct new ones. This conclusion is reinforced by the identification of coal reserves in the northern regions that could be developed to supply a 20 mw generating station.

R.S. Maya's study focuses on the potential for, and the barriers to, the use of coal as an alternative to biomass in rural areas of Zimbabwe. Based on a survey of rural households, he found no significant cultural barriers or resistance to the use of coal or coal stoves. Rather, he concluded that cost and lack of exposure to the new technology are the significant barriers. In order to overcome these barriers, it was recommended that coal be supplied in bulk to centres in the user districts and that purchasers be able to buy coal over a continuous range of quantities. The government should also consider removing the sales tax on coal for certain households. The study is notable for directly confronting health and environmental issues arising from greater use of coal as a household fuel. While the dangers are relatively low, public education will be essential to prevent improper combustion of coal in open fires or use of hazardous stoves. Further, care will have to be taken with the disposal of coal ash, which risks polluting water and soil with heavy metals.

M. P. Modisi assessed the coal resource base in Botswana against present and potential future demand. Coal reserves in Botswana are very large, and annual production now exceeds half a million tonnes. In the past attention focused on export potential but current production is mainly for electrical generation and heavy industry. Recently, a campaign has been launched to stimulate the substitution of coal for woodfuel and petroleum products in government institutions, households and small industry. Future developments in coal-fired electrical generation depend as much on the availability of water for cooling as on the development of new markets. However, the most likely next site at Mmamabula does have a water supply and is close enough to the main population centres to offer a viable source of supply for household, institutional and light industrial use.

A.N. Ng'andu investigated the influence of comparative price on the rate of substitution of coal for woodfuel and charcoal in Zambia. Although nationally Zambia is not experiencing a problem, in urban areas and in the copper belt fuelwood and charcoal shortages are beginning to appear as a result of excessive wood harvest and land clearance. Using both a literature search and interviews, Mr. Ng'andu collected data to identify the market structures for charcoal and coal, and to build an economic model of coal and charcoal use. (Currently, the prices of both charcoal and coal are controlled by the government with the former used mainly by households and the latter mainly by industry.) Regression equations for the quantity of charcoal purchased showed that only population was a significant variable, and that use was relatively inelastic. Cross-elasticities with the price of coal were also measured but were not stable from year to year. They do however suggest that the markets for coal and charcoal are rather separate and that the price of charcoal has to rise signficantly before a threshold is reached at which households will switch to coal. Accelerating this switch would require parallel policy measures involving housing structures, fuel pricing and incomes. A switch to electricity may, under the circumstances, be more feasible and more economic.

Oil and natural gas

In Africa, the use of ethanol as a partial substitute for petrol in powering motor vehicles was pioneered by Zimbabwe and followed by Kenya. But the idea of replacing kerosene by ethanol in cooking stoves is still a novel one and has not progressed beyond the laboratory experimental stage: J. Baguant and his colleagues in Mauritius have conducted technical and techno-economic research into this possibility. The sugar industry in Mauritius generates enough molasses, in principle, to produce all the ethanol required for entirely replacing imported kerosene. Ethanol cooking stoves imported from Sweden have been tested and local adaptations of them have been designed. Comparison of the thermal efficiencies of kerosene and ethanol stoves, as well as of the retail price of kerosene and the production cost of ethanol, show that the ethanol stove is quite competitive. With a population of about one million, the substitution, if carried out, could result in a net foreign exchange saving of about 3 per cent of the total energy import bill of Mauritius.

Baguant and his colleagues seem confident that the power output and technical efficiency of their modified ethanol stoves can be further improved. Such improvements, if linked to more efficient production of ethanol from molasses and appropriate pricing policies, could make ethanol a really attractive alternative to kerosene. However, before such a policy can even be contemplated, the problem of how to dispose of vinasse, the by-product of ethanol production from molasses, must be resolved in an environmentally sound way: some theoretical possibilities are the use of vinasse as a fertiliser and as a substitute for furnace fuel.

Any country that wants to promote national control over the petroleum sector within its own borders must necessarily institute policies and strategies for the acquisition of a range of technical and managerial skills by its nationals. Tanzania committed itself to this task in the late 1960s through the establishment of the state-owned Tanzanian Petroleum Development Corporation (TPDC). M. Mwandosya describes the process whereby TPDC promoted the acquisition of capabilities in negotiating contracts in marketing, exploration and production, which he regards as being essential. These negotiating skills spanned a wide range involving petroleum economics, legal matters, national sovereignty, petroleum geology, geophysics, geochemistry, etc.

The formative years of this strategy were between 1973 and 1977, when TPDC learnt how to collect, process and analyse information, monitored marketing activities of oil multinationals and their Tanzanian subsidiaries, and acquired knowledge of the working of the international oil industry. It was helped in this by the state-owned oil sectors in India and Norway. Mwandosya quotes the striking example of how the skills it had so acquired enabled TPDC to bypass the local subsidiaries of oil multinationals and become the sole importer of crude oil. A major instrument used effectively by Tanzania to enhance the transfer of technical and managerial knowledge was to incorporate clauses on the employment of nationals and their training in the agreements signed with foreign subsidiaries.

Institutions and planning

The extremely high economic and social costs imposed by the dependence on imported crude oil and refined petroleum products have prompted African governments to find ways of reducing the consumption of these imported fuels without grievously harming their economies. This calls for the management of demand not only in petroleum, but also in other fuels, both modern and traditional, because of the interconnection between, and the inter-sectoral impact of, different forms of fuel. Workable measures for regulating energy demand on a national basis cannot be arrived at without appropriate planning and institutional mechanisms. Three papers in this volume deal with several aspects of planning and institutions within the contexts of Ethiopia, Kenya and Lesotho. A fourth paper, written in the Seychelles, analyses the usefulness of existing energy models to energy planners and policy-makers in general.

Kenya displays the imbalances in the energy picture typical of many countries in the region. P.M. Nyoike and B.A. Okech point out that petroleum accounts for nearly 85 per cent of the modern forms of energy used in Kenya, electricity for 12 per cent and coal for the remaining 3 per cent. Petroleum and coal are wholly imported. The bulk of the electricity comes from domestic hydro-electric and geothermal sources, with 10 per cent being imported from Uganda. Petroleum ought therefore to be the prime candidate for demand management in the modern energy sector. Despite formal development planning exercises since 1968 and the creation of a Ministry of Energy in 1979, energy policy-making has been piecemeal at best and energy planning quite fragmented. For instance, pricing is the only major instrument that has been tried seriously so far in curbing petroleum use. Nyoike and Okech argue that in order to arrive at measures for effective demand management, including energy conservation in the industrial sector, one needs to analyse and assess the following factors: constraints and potential capabilities of existing institutional structures; interests of end-users; conditions for making capital available for investment; technologies in use; attitudes to, and practices in, recruiting, training and deploying key personnel.

It is the last factor mentioned above, i.e. the training of personnel, that concerns M. Lebesa and L. Mohapeloa. They begin by noting that a large number of foreign-funded development projects in Lesotho have failed. They attribute this, among other things, to the fact that local people, who had to take over from departing expatriate project personnel, had not acquired the required training. Their research uncovers three main reasons for this state of affairs. Firstly, projects are designed by foreign donor agencies without adequately involving local officials in the process. A large share of the responsibility for this lapse lies with the Lesotho authorities, for the government is often unable to find and assign local counterparts. Secondly, the government does not sufficiently keep track of the projects to make sure that the training schemes built into them are actually being carried out to agreed schedules. The inadequate implementation of the training component surfaces once the expatriate personnel have handed over the projects to local personnel. Thirdly, the career and remuneration structures available to nationals after acquiring their training are not conducive to retaining them on the projects.

Based upon their findings, Lebesa and Mohapeloa make a number of policy recommendations whose central thrust is that the details of the training schemes should be clearly worked out in advance; national counterparts should be assigned to the projects at the very start and their training closely monitored; and the nationals so trained should be obliged to stay on till the projects have been fully implemented, with adequate salary and promotion incentives designed to that end.

As J. Morgan points out in his analysis of available types of energy models which can be handled on a microcomputer, they are tools which can help the planner and the policy-maker by making their assumptions explicit, by providing consistency and by presenting various options. What they cannot do is to absolve the policy-maker of the responsibility of actually choosing between options and taking decisions. Morgan looks at three main types of models: the accounting framework type, the planning type and the reference systems type. The choice is governed by the nature of the task that the planner has to tackle. According to Morgan, available models are broad enough to process issues of policy, planning and project evaluation. He says that in the policy arena, the models can tackle fiscal, trade, environmental, commodity distribution, technology and resource questions. In the planning area, they can deal with supply and demand projections, resource allocations and social and economic trade-offs. In project evaluation, they can assess the impact of technologies, costs and benefits, the dynamics of energy outputs and economies of scale.

Mengistu Teferra reports on the use of a particular model to forecast energy demand in Ethiopia. The central feature of the model, which was originally developed in the context of Bangladesh, is the use of energy intensity per unit of sectoral GDP. The major consumers of electricity, petroleum and biomass in Ethiopia are respectively the manufacturing industry, transport and household sectors. Although the national development plan guidelines did not specify the sectoral GDP growth rates, these were derived through regression analysis of past trends in the relative magnitudes of sectoral GDPs. Based on these estimates of trends and applying the criterion of energy intensity per unit of sectoral GDP, the future demand in electricity, petroleum and biomass was computed. While these forecasts may in themselves be quite useful as pointers to the direction in which to move, Mengistu Teferra quite correctly points out the limitations built into them through the simplifying assumptions on the continuity of past trends and the inaccuracies in sectoral GDP forecasts. Further, the model does not take into account the impact of inter-fuel substitutions. Nor does it deal with energy conservation and other measures for energy demand management.

2 Renewable Energy Technologies

2.1 New Approaches to the Development and Utilisation of Renewable Energy Resources in Uganda

Salim A. Bachou

Background

The national economy

Uganda's economy is basically agricultural, exhibiting a great preponderance of subsistence farming. Agricultural exports are dominated by coffee, which accounts for more than 90 per cent of total export earnings. Cotton, tobacco and food crops account for the rest. Frequent vicissitudes in international trade, particularly in commodity terms of trade detrimental to primary sector exports, have imposed an adverse balance of payments on Uganda for the last several years. Its debt service ratio is about 60 per cent.

Uganda's manufacturing sector has been systematically destroyed over the years by prolonged economic mismanagement, accompanied by the political euphoria which characterised the 'Economic War' era (declared by the Idi Amin government in the 1970s). Mining has experienced the same fate, and so have tourism and other service sectors. Attempts by successive political regimes to revitalise the economy have so far achieved modest results, although there is a glimpse of hope in this regard, if the relatively stable current political environment could be maintained.

The energy sector

Given this background, it was not to be expected that the energy sector would do any better. Indeed, the energy sector, alongside economic infrastructure like roads and other communication systems, manifests the worst symptoms of sustained neglect. During the period 1980—85, Uganda's energy 'production' grew at 3.3 per cent per annum, compared to a consumption growth rate of 5.2 per cent. While these figures relate to total energy use, it is imperative to remember that at least 92 per cent of Ugandans depend for all their energy requirements on woodfuel, a subsector that has not witnessed any growth for several years. On the contrary, continuous uncontrolled depletion of Uganda's wood reserves has inflicted severe deforestation on some parts of the country. Also, the growth in energy 'production' includes oil imports.

On balance, Uganda's demonstrated energy deficiency is startling, given its observed energy potentials in both commercial and non-commercial sub-sectors. Energy sources of interest include biomass, hydro-power, geothermal, solar and wind energy. As for petroleum products, the country imports all its requirements, accounting for at least 50 per cent of total foreign exchange imports. In a typical fiscal year, Uganda imports 260 million litres of assorted petroleum products, of which 69 per cent are in the form of petrol and diesel for the transport sector, 17 per cent for the household sector, 9 per cent for aviation, and 5 per cent for industrial use. Total electricity generated in 1986 was 636.8 million kwh, some of which was exported to Kenya.

As already noted, the overall potential for the development of indigenous energy resources in Uganda is quite high, although they remain largely unexploited. For example, an estimated 374,000 tonnes of coffee husks are produced annually. Of this amount, an estimated 40 per cent is used as manure on banana plantations, leaving a balance of 224,000 tonnes that could be used in other forms such as charcoal briquettes. This quantity could replace 50 per cent of the fuelwood used annually in the country to produce charcoal. It is estimated that biogas from a national cattle population of approximately 4 million head could meet the cooking and lighting needs of at least 3 million families in Uganda. The national hydro-power potential is about 2,000 mw. Of this, only 152 mw have been exploited. A United Nations Development Programme (UNDP) study completed in 1971 estimated that Uganda's geothermal energy potential, which has not yet been exploited, is in the region of 450 mw. In addition, Uganda has abundant solar energy potential which has not been exploited fully.

Fuelwood

Available data indicate that Uganda consumes its energy in the following forms: firewood (92 per cent); charcoal (4 per cent); petroleum, electricity and others (4 per cent). Consumption by sector is divided into household (80 per cent), commerce (12 per cent), industry (5 per cent), passenger transport and other (3 per cent). In view of the predominance of woodfuel in Uganda's energy sector, the country is now faced with a crisis in terms of a serious imbalance in woodfuel supply and demand. The present rate of depletion in the woodfuel sub-sector is estimated to be 17 per cent above the sustainable yield per annum. In 1983, consumption of woodfuel was estimated at 13.6 million tonnes, against a projected sustainable yield of 10.9 million tonnes, or 75 per cent of the requirement. These figures indicate that without concerted efforts in wood energy conservation, supported by the development and use of woodfuel substitutes, the present crisis could scale up to a disaster by the turn of the century. This is the crux of the energy sector problem.

Evidently, the key to ameliorating this problem lies in reducing the demand for wood-based fuel, while increasing its supply through tree planting and conservation of existing woodfuel reserves. This can be achieved largely by providing alternative sources of energy to woodfuel, even if its supply remain constant in the short run, and by developing devices which would use woodfuel more economically.

Government and local NGO activities in the woodfuel sub-sector

Government-supported activities

The uncontrolled harvesting of Uganda's wood energy reserves has been little publicised. Nonetheless, the present administration has found it imperative to create a ministry especially to cater for environmental affairs and, of course, a separate Ministry of Energy has been carved out of the Ministry of Power, Transport and Communication — in part to address the same issues as the Ministry of Environment Protection. Thus far, the Ministry of Energy has addressed itself to the question of fuelwood consumption in two industries which depend almost entirely on fuelwood for their energy requirements — tobacco curing and brick and tile production.

In tobacco curing, the UNDP/World Bank Energy Sector Management Assistance Programme (ESMAP) has identified measures to conserve fuelwood using BAT (Uganda) Ltd as an implementation agency under the auspices of the Ministry of Energy. ESMAP's pilot projects in the West Nile Region (Arua District) have demonstrated that efficiency improvements of between 40 and 80 per cent can be achieved through the use of improved tobacco-curing barns. These pilot projects were implemented during 1986–87. This attempt is now being emulated in other tobacco-growing parts of the country. ESMAP has also identified efficiency improvement measures in the brick and tile industry. A pilot project is expected to test these measures in the near future. The Commonwealth Science Council projects in Uganda have experimented with solar crop drying (coffee and cereals), biogas production and utilisation, and charcoal production. But these endeavours have been little publicised and, therefore, not replicated on a wider scale.

All these efforts, commendable as they no doubt are, cannot achieve the desired balance in the supply and demand of fuelwood in Uganda. They must be supported by large-scale tree planting activities at institutional level, like those BAT (Uganda) Ltd is undertaking in Arua District. With support from the company, tobacco farmers in Arua District have over the years been creating their own reserves of eucalyptus trees for use as firewood in the industry. The Ministry of Energy is also planning to conduct a survey of urban household energy use with financial support from the World Bank. It is hoped that this survey will provide reference material for policy design in the energy sector.

Local NGO activities

Aware of the limited government initiatives in woodfuel conservation, and in the absence of explicit and wide-ranging government policy in this area, a number of local non-governmental organisations (NGOs) and quasi-NGOs have embarked on selected woodfuel conservation activities. Among them are USIKA Crafts, JEEP (Joint Energy and Environment Projects), Black Power (U) Ltd, YWCA, Wildlife Clubs of Uganda, and Boy Scouts of Uganda.

The main areas of local NGO activities in the energy sector include:
- a national problems awareness programme;
- a national tree planting campaign;
- a wood energy conservation programme revolving around improved cooking stoves and kitchen energy management; improvements in wood-burning industries (especially brickmaking) and charcoal production; and development of woodfuel substitutes, particularly residue fuel.

Major bottlenecks

All the NGOs involved in the drive to conserve woodfuel and to increase its supply are confronted with one principal obstacle — that of scale. Their inputs, whether in information dissemination or in the production of cooking stoves, are negligible. The result is that the impact of their efforts is limited to very small segments of the population in major urban centres. Yet the problem spans the whole country, with the most dissipating effects in the rural areas.

In turn, the problem of scale is caused by inadequate finance, inadequate material support, and to some extent by poor organisation and limited co-operation between the NGOs and other institutions. To address the issue of co-ordination, key local NGOs, with government policy support, established an umbrella non-governmental agency known as Uganda National Energy Development Organisation (UNEDO). UNEDO is expected to address:
- the need to streamline the operational bottlenecks of organisations involved in energy-sector activities;
- the need to fill the technical manpower gap in the Ministry of Energy; and
- the need to attend to observed energy sector problems in a more systematic and effective fashion.

Conclusions

This study is oriented towards policy formulation and implementation. It seeks to provide an institutional framework for masterminding and spearheading research, project identification, planning and implementation covering major aspects of renewable energy resources in Uganda. Its principal propositions are encapsulated in a number of suggestions/recommendations, a summary of which is provided below.

- In view of the perceived threat to Uganda's biomass resources, accompanied by potential ecological and environmental problems, it is recommended that residue fuel of assorted categories be developed as a matter of priority, supported by serious tree planting throughout the country. The development of biomass-derived residue fuel requires a costing study to assess the magnitude of capital outlays involved.
- In spite of Uganda's huge potential for big hydro-electric power plants, it

is recommended that preference be given to mini/micro hydro-electric power plants for which the potential is equally sizeable, on account of capital outlay considerations and the desire for decentralised development propelled by the private sector. For this purpose, it is suggested that a cost-benefit study be undertaken based on selected cross-country experiences to lend further support to this proposition.
- Given the lack of information about Uganda's geothermal energy potential, there is a need to conduct surveys and explorations to determine this potential.
- Uganda should encourage and support the application of solar energy devices for use by rural institutions such as schools and health centres.
- The recently established Uganda National Energy Development Organisation (UNEDO) should be given financial and material support to warrant its institutional development and to accord it the opportunity to implement its programme of activities through its associate members and private sector organisations.

The burden of considering and implementing those policy recommendations lies with the government. However, donor agencies and NGOs have an important role to play. For example, donor agencies could consider funding the following:

- a study to determine cost-benefit comparisons between major and mini/micro hydro-electric plants;
- a study to assess the status and use of renewable energy resources in Uganda;
- institutional development of Uganda National Energy Development Organisation (UNEDO);
- projects conceived by UNEDO, among which are: (1) production of improved cooking stoves and briquettes; (2) improved kiln for tobacco curing, brickmaking and charcoal production; (3) installation of biogas demonstration plants and small solar systems; and (4) training of artisans in assorted skills.

2.2 Review of Mature Renewable Energy Technologies in Sub-Saharan Africa

Stephen Karekezi

Renewable Energy Technologies (RETs) have, in the eyes of many, failed to fulfil their promise. In the early 1970s, RETs were seen as a panacea for sub-Saharan Africa's deteriorating energy situation. They were perceived as a low-cost and appropriate alternative to conventional energy technologies — appropriate, above all, for use by the rural and urban poor of Africa.

Over the last 15 years, significant financial resources were invested in RET projects, yet today RETs continue to face daunting hurdles. A large number of RETs are beyond the financial reach of their principal target groups, the rural and urban poor of sub-Saharan Africa. Other RETs were not tailored to user needs. RETs that *are* low-cost continue to face enormous problems, whether of support at the policy level or of large-scale dissemination at the end-user level.

Despite these obstacles, a number of RETs have demonstrated an unexpected level of success in the early 1980s. The objective of this study is to examine in detail relatively successful experiences in the development of a number of RETs in sub-Saharan Africa. The approach is based on case studies of each RET, backed by an intensive survey of the literature. For windpumps, the study reviews the experience of the Kenya 'Kijito' windpump project which received significant technical assistance from ITDG of the UK. The case study on micro-hydro systems examines the experience of a USAID-funded project in Madagascar which supported the installation of a 64 kw micro-hydro station in Ampefy in the island's central province. The nascent photovoltaic industry in Kenya is the setting for the case study on solar energy devices.

For wood energy technologies, two major case studies, both dealing with essentially the same RET — improved cooking stoves — are reviewed. The first examines the Lesotho 'Mabotle' project while the second assesses the experiences of the well-known Kenya Ceramic Jiko (KCJ) project. The most detailed treatment is reserved for discussion of the above two case studies. Improved cooking stoves are a well-understood RET and almost all sub-Saharan countries have attempted to tackle the problems of deforestation and household energy by encouraging the wide-scale introduction of energy-efficient stoves.

The case studies provided the research with an opportunity to examine the fundamental research and policy questions that face the development of RETs in sub-Saharan Africa. Within the regional context, and with special reference to the two improved cooking stove case studies, the research project determines the importance of the factors discussed below in determining the success of RETs.

Base-line information on renewable energy resources

The Lesotho improved stove and Kijito windpump case studies illustrate how the absence of adequate base-line data on energy resources and consumption patterns has hobbled initiatives to promote the use of improved cooking stoves and other RETs in the region.

As confirmed by the case studies, the majority of donor-funded RET projects last an average of two to three years. Faced with rapidly approaching completion dates, most RET project managers elect not to undertake lengthy and costly renewable energy surveys that would yield a host of renewable energy data maps and resource information but little or no short-term and tangible benefits. As might be expected, most RET project managers resort to rapid country appraisals which are clearly inadequate.

Although the availability of base-line information would greatly assist the development of RETs in sub-Saharan Africa, it does not appear to be a critical factor that can make or break an RET programme. As shown in the KCJ and Ampefy (Madagascar) micro-hydro case studies, base-line information provided an important source of data to support the initiatives within policy circles, but the importance of this support was peripheral. It was not a prerequisite in the success of both the KCJ and Ampefy projects.

Coherent national energy policy guidelines for the development of RETs

Energy planning instruments capable of identifying the appropriate niche for RETs were not available in sub-Saharan Africa in the 1970s, nor have they been firmly established as yet. The Lesotho and Madagascar case studies illustrate this fact. Even in Kenya, where significant energy planning work has been undertaken, planning and policy guidance for further development of RET stoves is still lacking. Other countries in the region appear to be no better off. Thus the development and promotion of RETs was and continues to be undertaken within an 'energy planning and policy vacuum'.

Within the RET field, there was and still is little guidance on what technology should be given priority. Your typical RET project manager in sub-Saharan Africa had at the outset no idea as to whether to focus on micro-hydro, solar or wind. He therefore was compelled to carry out rapid country reviews, scattering efforts and resources by undertaking a wide range of RETs. Some RET projects had no less than ten technologies at various stages of development and dissemination. Often the ironic result was that by the time the RET project manager had gained a good understanding of energy needs and identified the most promising technologies, his project would be approaching its end.

Policy support for RET research in sub-Saharan Africa has typically been available when there are ongoing donor-funded projects, or when there are prospects of external support. RETs have seldom enjoyed sustained support from the design stage through to dissemination. The KCJ and Madagascar case studies are typical examples.

Whenever external support for an RET project ceases, and management and budgetary responsibility is transferred to local entities, luke-warm policy support usually causes the project to grind to a halt in a short time. The Mabotle stove programme is a typical example.

As with the base-line information factor, it appears that the provision of policy guidelines is important to the development of RETs in sub-Saharan Africa. But, as shown by the KCJ case study, policy is peripherally rather than centrally important to the development and promotion of RETs.

Research, technical and maintenance skills

Most RET projects in the region share one major characteristic — the almost total absence of senior and well-qualified local researchers. The Mabotle stove project is the classic example, while the KCJ stove project shows what one can achieve if a minimum number of local researchers are identified and/or trained.

The low level of technological development in most sub-Saharan African countries also adversely affects RET projects. Most external agencies overestimate the engineering capability of host country institutions and target groups. Lack of spare parts and poor maintenance continue to plague almost every RET, giving rise to the rather depressing sight of abandoned and inoperative windpumps and solar installations.

The weak technological infrastructure of most countries in the region leads to the development of RETs largely outside the existing manufacturing sector. As a result, most RET projects are unable to link into the dynamic informal/cottage industrial sector which exists in most sub-Saharan countries. The Ampefy micro-hydro case study is a typical example. Those RET projects that are able to establish a link with the existing manufacturing sector, whether in the formal or informal sector (e.g., the KCJ project), register a more encouraging level of success.

In contrast to the factors of base-line information and policy guidelines, which are important but not vital, it appears that the presence of adequate research, technical and maintenance skills is absolutely essential to the development of RETs in sub-Saharan Africa.

Wide-scale dissemination and commercialisation strategies

The other main constraint faced by most RET projects in the region is that of wide-scale dissemination. As mentioned above, a number of RET projects prematurely jumped to the dissemination phase prior to carrying out a comprehensive survey and assessment of user needs. Some of the RETs were still at the research and development level when attempts were made to promote them (e.g., the Mabotle stove).

But even well-proven RETs face enormous difficulties in ascending to the phase of wide-scale dissemination. Developing an efficient and less costly RET device is not nearly as difficult as ensuring that it reaches its target population which, in the case of household energy devices, is measured in millions. Wide-scale dissemination calls for a whole range of skills and a longer time-scale than that provided by most RET projects.

Ability to harness the positive energies of the commercial sector is likely to determine the long-term prospects of RETs in sub-Saharan Africa. Most RET projects pay very little attention to the importance of ensuring attractive financial returns that would entice the local private sector (formal and informal) into committing their own capital to RET technology development and dissemination. This is illustrated by the Mabotle stove programme. In most successful RET projects, such as the KCJ project, attractive financial returns seem to have played a crucial role in ensuring sustainable development.

Evidence from both the Mabotle and KCJ case studies seems to indicate that appropriate dissemination and commercialisation strategies are critical to the successful development of RETs.

Conclusions

The following table, which is limited to the two case studies on cooking stoves, summarises the relative importance of various factors to the success of RETs in sub-Saharan Africa.

Table 1

Factor	KCJ Programme	Mabotle Project
Base-line information on renewable energy resources	Important, particularly in the early phases	Important but not critical
Coherent national energy policy guidelines for the development of RETs	Important but more so in the later phases of the programme	Important but not critical
Research, technical and maintenance skills	Very important, major contributor to the success of the KCJ programme	Absence largely responsible for failure of project
Wide-scale dissemination and commercialisation strategies	Absolutely essential, key determinant of success	Another major reason for failure

The RET research agenda

The relatively successful RET projects that one can identify in sub-Saharan Africa are at a crossroads. Over the last few years, RET activities have increasingly shifted towards adoption of labour-saving machinery which entails a dramatic change of scale of operation. Large-scale dissemination on an industrial scale seems to be the next logical step. As might be expected, problems of quality control and marketing have arisen.

Researchers who were instrumental in the early success of these RETs are uncertain as to what type of research is necessary at this stage. The second phase of this study will address the following questions:

- What are the research strategies that will ensure continuous growth of these RETs and maintain the support of key interest groups: policy-makers, the private sector, non-government organisations (NGOs) and end-users?
- Are these strategies applicable to the region?
- Which research institutions are most suitable for the above tasks?
- What should be the role of NGOs, policy-makers and the private sector in RET research?
- Should research shift from design to production, engineering and marketing? If so, on which particular aspects should research concentrate?

2.3 Solar Hot Water for Household and Institutional Use in Bujumbura, Burundi

Joseph Katihabwa

Solar energy is clean and renewable. It is the primary source for a wide range of energy resources such as biomass, hydraulics, coal, peat and petroleum. Until recently, the sun was the major source of energy used by man to satisfy his needs. The extraction and use of fossil fuels became important with the technological and industrial development that took place in the nineteenth century.

For countries without fossil fuels (such as petroleum and coal), solar energy is an important asset. The oil crisis of 1973 clearly showed the limits of fossil fuel consumption. The crisis slowed down and, in some cases, severely hampered economic growth in many developing countries. To this day, fossil fuels remain expensive for many developing countries which have to part with a significant share of their meagre convertible currency resources to import fossil fuels.

It is thus imperative that developing countries should investigate the possibility of developing solar energy systems that can reduce their dependence on fossil fuels. In the short term, high investment costs and shortage of qualified manpower are major constraints on the development of solar energy systems. In the long run, however, the benefits of solar energy systems are expected to overcome these constraints. The benefits include low operation costs and non-generation of pollutants.

The decentralised nature of solar energy is an asset in the isolated rural areas of Africa. It is possible to build small solar units and thus provide energy security and autonomy at the level of a community and even at the level of an individual.

Solar energy has, however, one major disadvantage — its energy density is low (1.0 kw per square metre on the earth surface, after taking absorption losses into account). The low density of solar energy is due not only to absorption losses incurred in the terrestrial atmosphere, but also to the earth's rotation and the long distance between the earth and the sun.

The low density of solar energy is a major handicap. It necessitates the use of extensive energy collection and some form of concentration system. The irregularity of solar energy is another handicap. As a result, energy storage equipment is often an essential part of solar energy systems.

The working principle of a solar water heater

There are now many countries with a wide variety of solar energy collectors.

The table below classifies the collectors by temperature range.

Table 1
Classification of solar energy collectors

Range	Classification	Application
10–50°C	Very low temperature	Heating, air conditioning
40–50°C	Low temperature	Heating sanitary water, air conditioning
80–120°C	Average temperature	Distillation, refrigeration, production of mechanical energy
200–600°C	High temperature	Production of mechanical energy and electricity, production of industrial heat
Beyond 600°C	Very high temperature	Production of heat for various transformations

Hot water for domestic usage normally reaches temperatures approaching 50°C to 60°C. It is produced with an 'ordinary collector' which is a key component in the solar energy collection system. The ordinary flat plate collector is composed of the following parts:
- a box made of a metallic frame to secure the cohesion of the system;
- an absorber made of a black-painted metal sheet to transform energy into heat which is exchanged with the energy-transporting fluid;
- tubes to circulate the energy-transporting fluid;
- an insulator to the inside (lateral and back) of the box;
- one (or two) protection glass(es) on top of the box.

The utilisation of a flat collector is based on the well-known 'glass house effect'. Ordinary glass allows the visible portion of the solar spectrum to pass through it, but is practically opaque to infra-red radiation. By passing through the glass, the visible radiation heats the absorber plate and the air retained under the glass. The result is a release of infra-red radiation which is stopped by the glass from being reflected back into the atmosphere. Thus, heat under the glass is produced and the temperature of the absorber increases continuously. This is the 'glass house effect'.

The energy stored by the absorbent is transferred into the transporting fluid. The effectiveness of the transformation of solar energy into directly utilisable energy depends on the nature of the collector and on the temperature of the transporting fluid.

Solar energy potential in Bujumbura

Bujumbura is the capital of Burundi. It has about 280,000 inhabitants and a growth rate of 6 per cent. Bujumbura is situated in the west of the country on the shores of Lake Tanganyika between 3°23' and 3°24' of latitude south and 29°21' and 20°23' of latitude east. It is situated at an average height of 790 m. The average annual temperature of the air is 23.5°C, with an average of 24.2°C in January and 22.4°C in July. Humidity usually ranges from 70 per cent to 90 per cent, sometimes rising to 99 per cent.

Historical data and measurements taken during the course of this study indicate that Bujumbura has only two seasons: from November to February when solar radiation is 407.35 cal/cm^2/day, and from March to October when it rises to 431.29 cal/cm^2/day (see Table 2 overleaf).

Energy consumption for residential water heating

Energy consumption in Bujumbura varies according to the type of residential area. In the medium to high income zones, 15 to 20 per cent of household expenditure is devoted to water and energy bills. Electricity is used for lighting, refrigeration, TV, radio and domestic water heating. Many families in the middle to high income zones have an electric cooker or a small electric stove. In general, water heaters have a capacity of 40 to 80 litres which is heated to a temperature of 50°C to 60°C. Hot water is mainly used in the morning and in the evening for bathing. During the day, a limited amount of hot water is used for domestic purposes (cooking and cleaning). About 40 per cent of the expenditure on energy is for water heating.

In the low-income zones, 8 to 10 per cent of household expenditure is devoted to procurement of water and energy. Less than 6 per cent of families in low-income zones are connected to both water and electricity mains. About 80 per cent have neither. Their main energy source is wood or charcoal. Approximately 2.5 kg of charcoal is used per family per day. Of this quantity, about 30 per cent is used for water heating. The daily expenditure on charcoal purchases is in the region of 50 FBu.

A brief survey conducted by this study showed that nearly all the water used in hospitals, hotels and high-income households came from electric heaters and/or electric stoves. Some low-pressure gas (LPG) is used to heat water. In low-income households, the primary fuel for water heating is charcoal or wood. In bread shops, wood is the major source of energy. Recently, some bread shops have started to use peat as a primary source of energy. Industries such as the breweries (BRARUDI) and cotton mills (COTEBU) use imported fuel oil. Soap manufacturers and oil mills use waste products from their factories for the generation of energy.

The evaporation of one litre of water (1 kg) requires 1.5 kg of firewood and costs 13.3 Fbu (US$0.10). Hot water produced by electric water heaters is very expensive. A kwh of electricity costs 36 FBu (or US$0.20). Investment costs for water heaters are very high. Water heaters can cost between 80,000 and 120,000 FBu. If the electricity is supplied by a thermal power plant, then the energy losses incurred are enormous. About 4 kwh of gas oil equivalent is required to produce 1 kwh of electricity. Further losses are incurred in using

Table 2
Solar radiation statistics for Bujumbura

Month	Wind speed (m/sec) daily average, 1975–81		Average temp. (°C), 1964–81	Solar creating duration annual totals (in 1/1000)				Global radiation in cal/cm^2/day	
	Day	Night		1971–75	1975–81	1966–70	1961–65	1963–73	1975–81
January	2.0	1.4	23	1863	1821	1840	1865	410.3	418.6
February	2.1	1.3	22.9	1718	1628	1560	1624	402.7	412.4
March	2.1	1.4	22.9	2000	1807	1717	1795	430.0	431.6
April	2.0	1.2	22.9	1786	1755	1856	1776	422.7	425.7
May	2.3	1.8	23.2	2150	2087	2222	2208	439.7	430.3
June	2.7	1.8	22.7	2445	2599	2470	2643	444.3	436.6
July	2.9	1.8	22.5	2499	2793	2800	2596	428.6	410.1
August	1.1	2.2	23.2	2663	2567	8634	2456	430.5	420.4
September	2.8	1.8	23.6	2069	2055	2139	2096	427.2	454.4
October	3.1	1.7	23.6	2040	2094	2142	1836	427.3	454.8
November	2.4	1.5	22.4	1697	1709	1500	1478	398.6	417.8
December	2.0	1.3	22.9	1642	1688	1801	1717	417.8	408.8
Average	**2.5**	**1.6**	**23**	**2048**	**2050**	**2057**	**2007**	**423.3**	**426.8**

Solar Hot Water for Household and Institution in Bujumbura

the electricity to heat water.

Utilisation of solar water heaters provides a viable alternative to the costly and inefficient water heating systems reviewed above. The Department of Mechanical Engineering in the Faculty of Applied Science, University of Burundi has developed and tested a solar water heater of 1.3 square metres which produces just under 700 w of incident solar power. This is sufficient to heat 1 litre of hot water at 70°C per minute. The output depends on the orientation of the collector and the inclination angle of the solar collector.

Measurement of solar radiation in Bujumbura over a period of 10 years shows the average to be about 426 cal/cm^2/day or 17,848 kj/m^2. A typical family of 6 persons needs 180 litres of hot water per day. If the water is heated to 50°C, the energy needs of the households are in the region of 4,500 kcal or 18,810 kj. This requires a solar collector of 1.5 square metres with an efficiency of 70 per cent. The investment cost of such a collector is close to 80,000 FBu (or about US$500). The payback period is about 5 years. For a period of 5–10 years, the running or operating and maintenance costs of such a water heater are minimal.

An electric heater of similar cost will need a major overhaul after 3–4 years, in addition to electricity bills of approximately 8,000 FBu/month or 288,000 FBu (US$1900) over 3 years.

It can thus be concluded that not only is solar water heating a low-cost alternative to electric water heating, but it could play an important role in alleviating the energy needs of a large proportion of households in Bujumbura.

2.4 Effectiveness of Research and Policy on Rural Energy Technology and Applications

Dominic Mbewe

By definition renewable energy sources either are unlimited over time or have a replenishment rate which exceeds that of extraction. Wind, sun, biomass and water are some of the renewable sources of energy.

Renewable energy sources can be tapped by rural energy technologies. These are technologies which, if made to act upon renewable sources of energy, turn them into forms of energy of immediate use to people whose quality of life consequently improves. Examples of rural energy technologies are: solar water heaters, solar fish dryers, photovoltaics, biogas digesters, efficient kilns for charcoal production, efficient charcoal cooking stoves, hay baskets for 'cooking without boiling', mini-hydro power plants, windpumps, firewood stoves and so on.

In Zambia policy-makers appear to be interested in rural energy technology research, with its direct relevance to problems affecting communities living in rural areas. This interest is strengthened by the fact that application of rural energy technologies in rural areas is among those measures which are most cost effective under prevailing economic conditions. Yet developments in this field have been sluggish.

The objective of this research, therefore, is to identify factors which account for the lack of communication and a smooth working relationship between those who take policy decisions, on one hand, and implementers of research in rural energy technologies on the other. It also focuses its attention not only on the effectiveness of past and present energy policy research, but also on recommendations aimed at narrowing gaps and disparities between research and its application to real problems. Both advisers and those who take decisions on issues and policies related to energy have expressed concern on many occasions over research programmes which did not or still do not yield any practical application in the Zambian society. In short, policy-makers would like to see to it that research and policy on rural energy technologies are relevant to problems in rural areas.

The research project focused on the following rural energy technologies: efficient kilns for charcoal production; efficient charcoal stoves for household use; introduction of hay baskets in households for 'cooking without boiling'; windmills; solar water heaters; solar fish dryers; biogas digesters; coal briquetting; and geothermal applications.

Charcoal production

A large proportion of households in urban and peri-urban areas of major towns in Zambia rely on charcoal for cooking.

Charcoal consumption is one of the causes of deforestation and ecological degradation of the regions that serve as sources of charcoal for major urban centres. It is in recognition of this effect on the environment that ways and means must be found to reduce consumption.

An obvious solution would be substitution by electricity or coal briquettes. However, this would require substantial investments in appliances such as electrical stoves, and in other equipment such as transformers, cables and so on.

It is therefore necessary in the short run to consider least-cost measures of reducing charcoal consumption. These measures entail the use of low-cost technologies, quite a number of which can be of use in Zambia.

Traditional charcoal production

Traditional charcoal production involves the piling of wood into clamps of about 20 cubic metres which are later covered by soil which prevents complete burning of wood during the period when carbonisation takes place. The yield of these traditional kilns is low. It is therefore recommended that research be embarked upon to improve the efficiency of traditional methods.

Metal kilns

Metal kilns ('Mark V') have been experimented on in Zambia with a view to ascertaining their efficiency and economic viability. Their cycle time is five days and the yield is between 25 and 30 per cent by weight. These metal kilns have been found unsuitable for use in Zambia: they are difficult to transport during the rainy season and also too expensive. I would therefore recommend discontinuation of research into this technology.

Charcoal retort

The development of charcoal retort, the viability of which depends upon the marketing of some of its by-products such as oils and tars, was initiated by members of staff of the Department of Mechanical Engineering at the University of Zambia, particularly Professor Francis D. Yamba. External funding from the Commonwealth Science Council and other donor agencies was secured by the University for this research project.

University energy research policy on technologies such as this, which if found feasible would benefit people living in rural areas, is not clear. Researchers are not given incentives. Many would-be researchers shun projects of this nature because their results would not be published in internationally recognised scientific journals. I would strongly recommend formation of a co-ordination committee consisting of researchers and government officials to solve problems inhibiting the implementation of research on charcoal retort.

Brick kilns

In Kitwe, the second largest town in Zambia, Forest Production Research

Division has carried out experiments on brick kilns. None of these kilns have been diffused so far — either because the initiators were expatriates and their contracts have expired, or because research was externally funded and funds to take projects to diffusion level are not available.

I would recommend that local researchers be given incentives to embark upon research of this type, and that government should provide funds for these projects to ensure continuity in project implementation.

Diffusion of efficient charcoal stoves

Professor Yamba and other members of staff of the Department of Mechanical Engineering at the University of Zambia also initiated the development of efficient charcoal stoves.

Funds for diffusion of the project have been provided by NORAD, and the Department of Energy is playing a co-ordinating role between researchers and implementers of the project.

Windmill

Prospects for wind energy technology are not good because of low wind speeds in Zambia. It is recommended that further research on windmill design be undertaken for the purpose of identifying a model suitable for Zambian conditions.

The Department of Water Affairs in the Ministry of Lands and Natural Resources put into service about 100 windpumps, mainly in Central Province. Practically all these pumps are unserviceable due to lack of spare parts and maintenance facilities.

Zambia's experience with wind energy serves, perhaps, to illustrate a general point: that external donor agencies are always in a hurry to implement untested technologies in developing countries. Too often, this concern does not extend to what will happen to the project after some years. And external agencies are sometimes slow to heed advice from local people as to the best way of implementing the project. I am inclined, therefore, to suggest that the Zambian government should follow a clear policy of rejecting technical assistance and grants if incompatible with our research programme and policy on energy.

Solar energy

Recommendations have been made to the government that the Department of Energy should supervise projects relating to solar energy applications from design to implementation stages. The Department of Energy will set up a technical group whose task will be to: (1) select a design and adapt it to Zambian conditions; (2) construct different prototypes for testing; (3) invite representatives from industry to participate in the testing and final design;

(4) prepare final design instructions and drawings for an industrial partner; and (5) assist in the implementation programme and solve system operational problems.

Private organisations and individuals have installed some solar water heaters in Eastern Province. They seem to work well.

Solar fish drying

Solar energy technologies for drying fish in Zambia have great potential. Recommendations have been made to the government to place project supervision under the Department of Energy in order to ensure that research and policy on solar fish drying technologies are effective. Similar measures are being taken on application of photovoltaic cells.

Biogas technology

Diffusion of biogas digesters in Zambia is being carried out by the National Council for Scientific Research. Slowly and successfully this technology is becoming available in Zambia.

Coal briquetting

A coal briquetting project was initiated in 1979. The project was aimed at improving the utilisation of coal from Maamba Collieries Ltd. Unable to secure foreign aid or technical assistance, the Department of Energy and the National Council for Scientific Research have budgeted K3,500,000 for the purpose of setting up a pilot plant in 1989.

Rural electrification

The Department of Energy has recently initiated a ceramic electric stoves project to be researched and developed by the National Council for Scientific Research, and implemented with government funding.

Conventional electric stoves are so expensive that very few people can afford them, and consequently the rural electrification programme has slowed down. It is hoped that cheaper ceramic electric stoves will suit rural budgets better than the expensive conventional models.

Conclusions

The study identified the following major factors contributing towards the ineffectiveness of research and policy on rural energy technology and applications: (1) lack of co-ordination among scientists and those charged with the responsibility of implementing the results arising from research; (2) inadequate screening of foreign or technical aid which may be incompatible or have strings attached to it; (3) lack of incentives for research scientists; and (4) inadequate funding of projects by government.

The study recommends the following: (1) creation of a Ministry of Science and Technology; (2) increase of government funding for projects; (3) rejection of some foreign or technical aid; (4) minimal use of expatriate scientists whose departure on expiry of the contract brings about discontinuities in research; and (5) introduction of incentives in the form of consultancy fees to encourage research scientists.

3 Bio-energy

3.1 Rural–Urban Household Energy Use and Inter-relation in the Central Region of the Sudan

Ismail A.R. Elgizouli

Urban and rural household energy consumption accounts for the major part of total energy consumption in most African countries. It ranges between 50 and 70 per cent in African countries with medium per capita incomes and between 58 and 93 per cent in those with low per capita incomes. Satisfying household energy needs takes up a substantial portion of the income of the urban household, while in the rural areas much time and effort are spent collecting wood instead of in more productive activities.

Woodfuel meets over 85 per cent of household energy demand in most African countries. This high level of consumption will remain, irrespective of the country's per capita income: woodfuel will continue to play a major role in the economics of developing countries and especially in the living standards of both rural and urban poor. The two major issues which must be considered are whether the forest resources are going to meet the future demand for woodfuel and whether prices will remain affordable to the low-income groups.

The problem of woodfuel scarcity is faced by many people as wood resources continue to be depleted. The problem is aggravated by the impact of fuelwood gathering on the ecosystem. Excessive deforestation which results from this and other practices leads to environmental degradation and the decline of land productivity. It is only too well known that as the environment deteriorates rural people are the ones who suffer most. Faced with decreased crop and animal production they may be forced eventually to emigrate to towns. Such a situation has prevailed in the Sudan over the past two decades which witnessed several periods of drought.

This study deals with household energy issues with special reference to the Central Region in the Sudan. It assesses local resources in the region, analyses consumption patterns of both rural and urban households, and discusses poss ble solutions to the impact of current energy practices.

The Central Region

The Central Region lies between latitudes 15°12′N and 9°30′N, and longitudes 35°40′E and 31°35′E. The region consists of three provinces: Gezira, White Nile and Blue Nile. The total area of this region is 140,000 square kilometres, or 6 per cent of the total area of Sudan. About 20 per cent of the total population live in the region.

38 Bio-energy

The Central Region is economically the most important region in Sudan. In 1985/1986 it produced 62 per cent of the country's cotton, 68 per cent of its wheat, 88 per cent of sugar production, 47 per cent of the sorghum crop and significant quantities of groundnuts, sesame seeds and millet. The region contributed 36 and 40 per cent respectively to total industrial and 'value added' production.

The region is one of the main suppliers of fuelwood and charcoal to other regions, mainly Khartoum. It is also the main producer of hydro-power to the urban centres.

Biomass resources in the Central Region

The main biomass resources in the Central Region are wood, agricultural residues and animal waste.

The woody biomass supplies were estimated to be 4.4 million cubic metres in 1987. Official documents show that a total of 587,332 tons of wood and 183,719 tons of charcoal production were licensed during the same year in the Central Region. These quantities imply an annual allowable cut of 3.4 million cubic metres. The estimated supply for consumption, however, is 4.4 million cubic metres, and the result is that too many trees are destroyed each year.

Agricultural residues include cotton stalks, wheat and sorghum residues, and groundnut shells. An estimated 3.2 million toe (tonnes of oil equivalent) of residues are used for energy and other purposes in the region. This estimate was derived from area cultivated, crops grown and yield data.

Animal waste was estimated at 1.2 million toe, a figure derived from the size of animal herds. Only 158,000 tons were used for energy, the rest for other purposes.

Urban and rural household energy consumption

The National Energy Administration conducted a survey that covered 7,200 out of a total of 800,000 households in the Central Region. Only 6,300 household survey results were used to determine the energy consumption in the region and 900 households were rejected. Random samples of households in urban and rural areas in each province were selected. For each sample family size, the type of fuel used and its quantity were recorded. This was then divided by the total number of the people in that group (urban, rural) to obtain the per capita consumption by fuel by province for each of the population groups in urban and rural areas. The total household energy consumption for each fuel, and for each group — urban or rural — in each province was calculated.

The population estimates of the region were derived from the Third Population Census (1983) using 2.5 per cent annual growth rate. The total population of the region was estimated to be about 4,014,740 persons. Nearly 3.2 million persons (80 per cent) lived in rural areas while about 0.8 million (20 per cent) lived in urban areas.

The total consumption of household energy in the Central Region was calculated to be 2.162 million tons in 1987. More than 97 per cent of this was in the form of biomass (wood, charcoal, agricultural residues and animal waste).

Wood consumption by household totalled about 593,000 tons in the region, of which 87 per cent was in the rural and only 13 per cent in the urban areas. Charcoal consumption was about 481,000 tons out of which 77 per cent was consumed in the rural areas. About 870,000 tons of agricultural residues was the estimated consumption as energy in the region in 1987. More than 90 per cent of it was consumed in the rural areas. Animal waste consumption was about 157,000 tons of which about 92 per cent was in the rural areas.

On a per capita basis consumption among urban households (0.1869 toe) was lower than in the rural areas (0.2417 toe), since the urban people are heavily dependent on purchased wood and charcoal, unlike the rural families who have relatively easy access to free wood and agricultural waste. Wood consumption on a per capita basis was higher among rural than among urban families. Charcoal consumption, on the other hand, was higher among the urban families since it is a commercial commodity and relatively expensive.

Total petroleum products consumed in the household sector were about 62,000 tons and represented only 8 and 6 per cent in the urban and rural areas respectively. Electricity consumption in urban areas was no more than 6.7 per cent of total household energy consumption, and was insignificant in rural areas.

Impact and causes

The Central Region, like the rest of the Sudan, is heavily dependent on biomass as the principal source of energy. Because of the continuing depletion of wood resources the country in general and the Central Region in particular is bound to face an acute energy crisis in the near future if the present trend of resource management continues.

In the past rural consumers used to obtain their fuelwood requirements from their immediate surroundings. At present fuelwood has to be fetched longer distances from places where some natural vegetation still thrives. Unlike rural areas, urban centres have grown very fast during the last decade due to mass immigration from the drought-stricken countryside. This increases urban demand for fuelwood which in turn increases the pressure on limited resources.

Increasing demand for woodfuel in the urban centres encourages wood cutters and charcoal burners to clear large areas of forest which are then exposed to soil erosion and the arable land available to rural residents shrinks further.

The increasing demand for energy, particularly in the urban centres, has caused fuelwood to become an important article of commerce. In spite of commercialisation the production cost is very low and has remained stable over a long period. However, market prices are constantly increasing, thus creating a big gap between production cost and market price, only partly explained by the high cost of transportation.

Possible solutions and options

Household energy supplies will continue to be endangered for millions of people in both rural and urban areas unless certain actions are taken. The first step is policies to control forest exploitation, regulating fuelwood cutting so as to avoid over-exploitation. Plans and a programme should follow in the following areas:

1. Substitution by fuels such as kerosene and proper utilisation of agricultural waste to reduce the pressure on fuelwood. The work which has been started in technologies such as gasification and briquetting should be accelerated and intensified to meet part of the energy requirements, especially in the rural areas.
2. Afforestation programmes, community forests and the application of sustained production management to the existing forests through the involvement of the local people.
3. Introduction and dissemination of improved charcoal stoves. This may reduce the woodfuel demand remarkably, depending on the efficiency that can be achieved.

Summary

There is a clear indication that millions of people in both urban and rural areas of the Central Region are going to face an energy problem. In this region, as in most parts of northern Sudan, the forests are being depleted because wood consumption rates far exceed the allowable cut.

As a result there is a growing demand for agricultural residue and animal waste, especially in Gezira Province where there is a scarcity of wood. The other two provinces, White Nile and Blue Nile, will soon be in a similar position if the present rate of depletion of forest continues.

A detailed resource assessment for the Central Region is regarded as necessary to show the actual situation, especially for wood, so that strategic plans can be drawn up.

Market prices of woody biomass are very high compared with the low cost of production, making it a very profitable business: this is bound to increase the rate of deforestation.

The government should draw up and implement plans to slow down the depletion of the forest. A household strategy is also required, with the aim of increasing the biomass supply (at prices affordable to the household) by reforestation programmes, fuel substitution and conservation programmes.

3.2 Rural and Poor Urban Energy Situation in Rwanda

Pierre-Claver Karenzi

Rwanda is a small landlocked country surrounded by Zaire, Uganda, Tanzania and Burundi. Seven million people inhabit an area of 26,000 square kilometres — an average density of 270 people per square kilometre.[1] The population is evenly spread over the whole country. Less than 5 per cent of Rwandeese live in an urban area, mainly in the chief town of Kigali, which has some 250,000 people.

The source of energy used in the rural areas is mainly fuelwood, while in Kigali charcoal is currently used for cooking. The average energy demand per capita per year has been evaluated at 0.8 cubic metres of fuelwood,[2] while Rwanda's plantations were able to supply no more than 0.4 cubic metres per capita per year by 1985.[3] It should be noted that in Rwanda the few remaining areas of natural forest have to be protected because of the population pressure. So the fuelwood problem is a highly sensitive one in the country, particularly in the neighbourhood of Kigali where charcoal prices are climbing.

This study presents the situation, highlights the measures deployed in Rwanda by governmental and non-governmental organisations (NGOs) concerned with energy matters, and indicates some tendencies likely to be uppermost in the near future.

Data on the fuelwood crisis

In 1983, Rwanda's National Bureau of Study Projects (BUNEP), in collaboration with Ecole Polytechnique Fédérale de Lausanne (EPFL, Switzerland) issued an important report on the energy sector in Rwanda.[4]

With regard to rural energy matters, the report mentioned a huge deficit in fuelwood of 2.8 million cubic metres per year. A complete exhaustion of fuelwood plantations was forecast for 1985 as shown in Fig. 1.[5] The only way of avoiding this catastrophe was to allow an attack on natural reserves, the report concluded, while a wide-scale programme in improved cooking stoves and biogas plants had to be launched (Fig. 2). Equilibrium could be reached by 1992 after destruction of 60 per cent of the natural forests. Some 700,000 improved cooking stoves and 56,000 biogas plants had to be disseminated within five years to reverse the tendency — a highly optimistic expectation.[6] Although the threat is real, these calculations did not take into account the wood and crop wastes which are widely used for fuel in rural areas (Fig. 3).

Another cause for concern is the inadequate supply of charcoal, given the growing demand from low and medium income families in urban areas, and

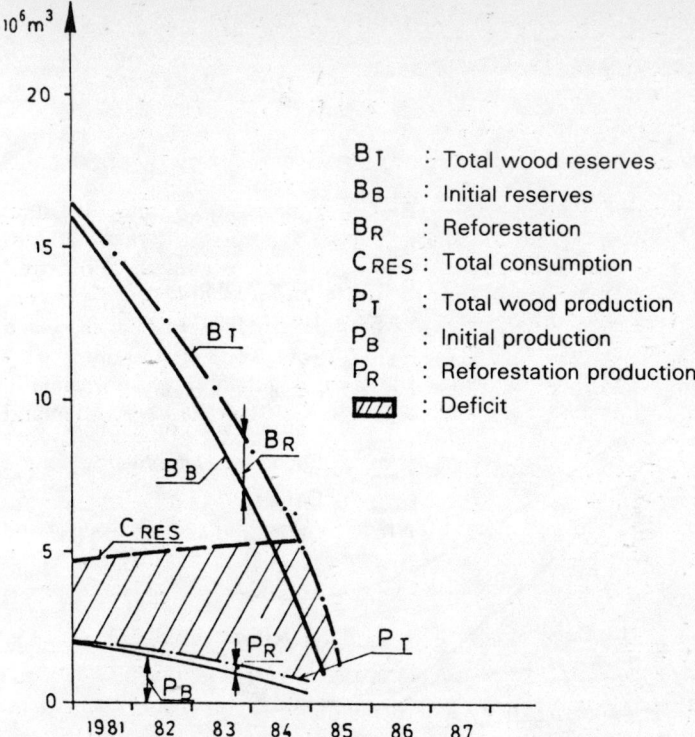

Figure 1. Wood reserves exhaustion

particularly in Kigali. Some 2,400 tons were consumed in 1977, mainly from natural savanna.[7] Today, available data estimate annual demand at more than 26,000 tons, 85 per cent of which comes from fuelwood plantations.[8] This shift in the supply base from natural reserves in the neighbourhood of the capital to the plantations makes the supply more and more distant, as shown by the map in Fig. 4. Obviously, this makes the charcoal more expensive.

Trends in solving the rural energy problem

Since 1974 many programmes have been started to reduce the pressure on fuelwood in Rwanda. A research centre (CEAER) has been founded at the National University of Rwanda to test and promote relevant suggestions regarding alternative energy resources. The centre has concentrated mainly on solar energy and biogas plants. CEAER staff have installed some 50 improved cooking stoves but have yet to undertake follow-up work.

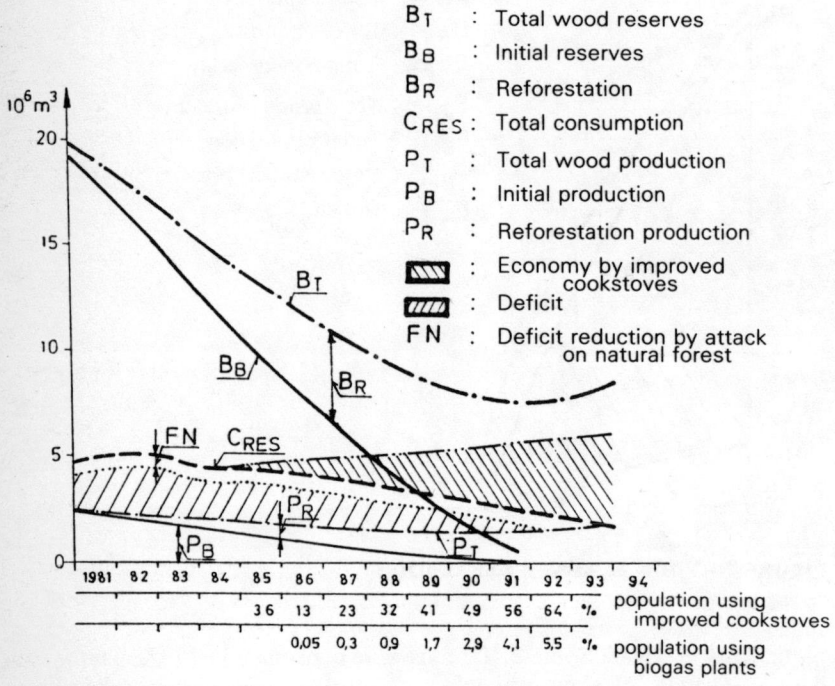

Figure 2. Deficit resorption by attack on protected reserves

In 1983, after the BUNEP/EPFL report was issued, the government elaborated a National Energy Policy[9] which covers the whole energy sector including fuelwood conservation by improved cooking stoves, reforestation and fuelwood substitution (briquettes and biogas), alternative energies (mainly methane gas from Lake Kivu) and solar energy. A planned electrical network would make the country self-reliant by the year 2000.

Steps to implement the National Energy Policy have been taken by the government with foreign assistance and by NGOs. Most notably, a reforestation programme started in 1978 had reached a tree planting rate of 19,000 ha/year by 1984. This successful progamme was in part a national

Figure 3. Evolution of firewood stock
  (a) **No crop wastes used**
  (b) **40 per cent of fuelwoods in crop wastes**

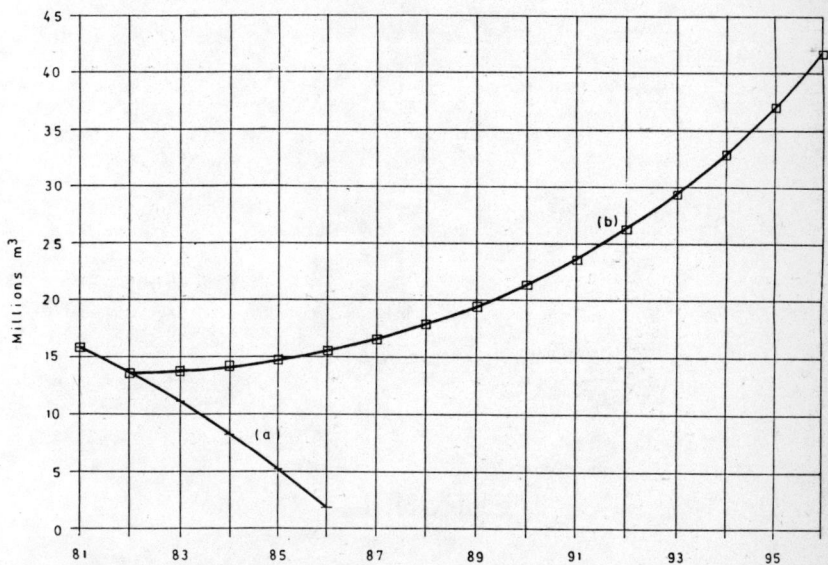

effort, with bilateral (Switzerland) and international (UNDP/WB) assistance.

Reforestation has been accompanied by an important programme of public education on the fuelwood and charcoal economy in rural areas, mounted with the help of NGOs (SNV, AFVP). Some 3,000 efficient stoves and improved charcoal burners are disseminated every year, mainly in the urban areas. A special programme has been started in primary schools to demonstrate efficient cooking stoves, while in high schools a course on alternative energy is part of general curricula in natural science options. All integrated rural development projects include a fuelwood saving aspect.[10]

Toward further progress

Most of the programmes mentioned above are quite new and — except for reforestation — have yet to make any visible impact in the rural areas. While they are under way, the real needs and uses of fuelwood in rural areas can be more closely considered. One particularly important factor is the contribution of wood and crop wastes.

A thorough analysis of the energy balance is planned through the African Energy Policy Research Network (AFREPREN), with the help of SAREC/

Figure 4. Charcoal supply for Kigali

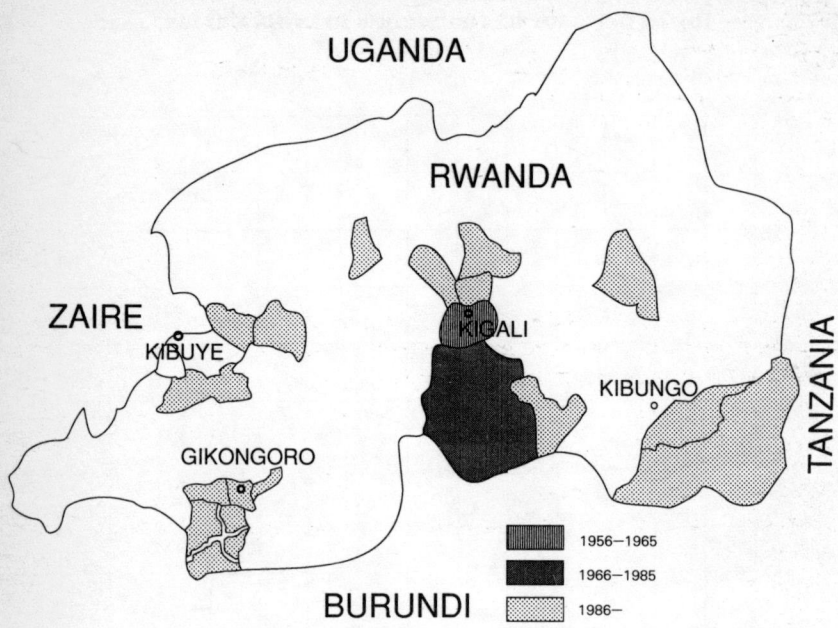

IDRC. We hope to get reliable data useful for relevant energy planning in Rwanda and other East and Southern African regions which also have wet climates and a high population density.

Notes

Acknowledgements
The detailed research summarised in this paper has been supported by the Canadian International Development Research Center (IDRC) and the Swedish Agency for Research Cooperation with Developing Countries (SAREC) through the National Institute of Developing Research and Documentation (NIR-Botswana). We are indebted to all these institutions for financial assistance without which this work could not have been completed.

The Rwandeese Ministry of Public Work and Energy has kindly provided us with valuable encouragement through its Direction Générale de l'Energie, Division des Energies Renouvelables. We hope that the research started in rural energy will make a modest contribution to solving the energy problem in Rwanda.

The National University of Rwanda has helped us by facilitating our participation in the Gaborone workshops and by providing access to its facilities. We are thankful.

1. Third Rwandeese National Plan for economic, social and cultural development, 1982–1986, p. 31.
2. Laurent Byamukama, *Besoins energétiques en milieu rural, mémoire de licence* (UNR, 1982).
3. Ministère de l'Agriculture, de l'Elevage et des Forêts, Direction Générale des Forêts, Plan Forestier National 1987–1997 (1987).
4. BUNEP/EPFL, *Etude du Secteur Energétique au Rwanda*, Vols I–VI, 1982–1983.
5. Ibid., Vol. V, p. 39.
6. Ibid., Vol. V, pp. 44, 52.
7. Frédéric Gatera, *Le bois et le charbon de bois dans la Commune Nyarugenge, mémoire de licence* (UNR, 1979).
8. Emmanuel Bahigiki, in ed. Shishazingucirwa, *Recueil des données sur les besoins en enérgie en rapport avec le milieu rural au Rwanda* (Butare, 1988).
9. Ministère des Ressources Naturelles, *Politique Energétique du Rwanda* (1983).
10. Pierre-Claver Karenzi, Emmanuel Bahigiki, Laurent Byamukama, Pascal Hakizimfura, Emile Karega and Frédéric Gatera, *Progress in Rural Energy Saving Programmes in Rwanda* (SAREC/IDRC, Butare, 1989).

3.3 A Critical Review of Fuelwood Surveys in Botswana

D. L. Kgathi

It is well known that developing countries are experiencing a second energy crisis, known as the fuelwood problem. The crisis takes the form of increasing scarcity of wood energy, particularly around the cities and large settlements of developing countries. In recent years, awareness of the fuelwood crisis — partly reflected by the proliferation of research on wood energy — has increased in many developing countries. In Botswana, interest in fuelwood research started in the 1980s. A number of fuelwood surveys have been undertaken since then.

There is general concern that some of the methods adopted in fuelwood surveys have flaws. Also, the results of a number of the surveys are not known to policy-makers, since they are scattered in a number of reports. A critical review of fuelwood surveys in Botswana is the object of this study.

The surveys: their objectives and focus

Seven surveys have been undertaken on socio-economic aspects of fuelwood in Botswana. The surveys can be divided into two groups: those commissioned by, or on behalf of, the government of Botswana; and those undertaken by the researchers at the National Institute of Development Research and Documentation (NIR).

In general, the surveys have addressed a range of issues, such as collection, distribution, marketing and consumption. Most surveys (71 per cent) focused on the fuelwood problem in the rural sector (Arntzen 1983; ERL 1985; Jelenic and Van Vegten 1981; Oki and Majaha-Jartby 1983). Of these, only two addressed issues pertaining to fuelwood use in such sectors as government, industry and commerce (Tietema et al. 1988; Oki and Majaha-Jartby 1983). The other surveys tended to concentrate on fuelwood issues in the household sector.

Among the surveys which addressed the rural fuelwood problem, the study on Energy Utilisation and Requirements undertaken by ERL (1985) was the most comprehensive. This study was commissioned by the UK overseas administration on behalf of the government of Botswana. It comprises two parts: the socio-economic, and the technical section which provides an assessment of biomass resources. The former section is of more relevance here. Among other things, it assessed the patterns and causes of energy demands, and the possibility of substituting traditional fuels with renewable sources of energy. Although the study covered many areas, they were all in the highly populated eastern part of Botswana.

Only 29 per cent of the surveys focused on the fuelwood problem in the urban sector. One examined fuelwood trade between the Kweneng district and the capital city of Gaborone (Kgathi 1984). This study was quite limited in geographical coverage since it was intended to be a pilot project.

Methodologies

Almost all of the fuelwood surveys in Botswana used probability sampling methods, and the samples were sufficiently large and therefore representative. The questionnaires had closed and open-ended questions. Inclusion of open-ended questions is considered to have many advantages, partly because 'it allows for flexibility and inclusion of the respondent's perceptions' (Morgan 1983). Most of the questionnaires were pre-tested in an attempt to improve the quality of the questions.

In all but a few surveys, the questionnaire method was supplemented by the informal personal interview approach. One of the advantages of the informal interview method is that it can sometimes enable the researcher to check the reliability of the information collected by the questionnaire method. This technique, known as triangulation (Abel et al. 1988), is very effective in improving the quality of data. The disadvantages of complete reliance on the questionnaire method are well known, and no attempt will be made to list them here. If the issue being investigated is a sensitive one, complete reliance on the informal interview method may be necessary, because the questionnaire method may not be rewarding.

In some surveys, the questionnaire was used to collect data on the distances travelled to points of fuelwood collection (Arntzen 1983; Tietema et al. 1988). If there are no budget and time constraints, it is not advisable to use the questionnaire for this purpose, because distance is rarely conceived in precise measurable terms by respondents, particularly the poor peasants in rural areas.

The other method of data collection used in some surveys in Botswana is that of observation. There are two modes of observation: participant and non-participant. The former is most used by anthropologists, and requires the researcher to take part in activities of the study population. The demerit of this method is that it is too demanding and requires a lot more time. Only one survey in Botswana utilised the method of participant observation. The main researcher lived in Oodi, which was one of the eastern Botswana study areas, where she participated in the activities of the local households, such as accompanying them on fuelwood collection trips (Jelenic and Van Vegten 1981).

In non-participant observation, the researcher does not become part of the study population. A number of socio-economic surveys in Botswana used the method of non-participant observation, particularly to assess the various uses of fuelwood (Gay and Zietlow 1983), and also to determine the manner in which labour was allocated to various activities, including fuelwood collection (Oki and Majaha-Jartby 1983).

Data was also collected by the method of fuelwood measurement. The method was used in 71 per cent of the cases, though it was not explained in some of the reports how the measurement was carried out (Gay and Zietlow 1983; Jelenic and Van Vegten 1981). Failing to explain fully the methodologies adopted in fuelwood surveys is a serious flaw, because it denies critical evaluation of how the findings were arrived at.

Most of the surveys used enumerators in the collection of data who were either secondary school leavers (Form IV) or students of the University of Botswana. In all cases, they were given basic training before they started the task of interviewing. There is evidence that supervision of the enumerators was inadequate in some surveys.

Patterns of fuelwood consumption

Fuelwood accounts for about half of the total energy consumption in Botswana. The ERL (1985) estimated the per capita consumption of fuelwood in rural Botswana to be 0.51 tonnes, or 0.57 cubic metres per year. On the other hand, Tietama et al. (1988) recorded a per capita consumption figure of 0.84 cubic metres in Dukwe, a relatively small settlement in the north-western part of Botswana. Per capita consumption of fuelwood was much lower in urban areas than rural areas. For instance, the per capita fuelwood consumption of Gaborone was estimated at 0.25 cubic metres per year, as compared with 0.49 cubic metres per year for Selibe Phikwe.

All socio-economic groups tended to use fuelwood for heating in winter, and, in areas where fuelwood was scarce, the rich peasants tended to use more fuelwood than the poor. Around urban areas and major agro-towns, fuelwood was used by all income groups for cooking, although the number of users was inversely related to socio-economic status. The percentage of the high income group using fuelwood was higher in the agro-towns (90 per cent) and much lower in the urban areas (10 per cent).

Fuelwood is also used in government, industrial and commercial sectors. In the government sector, it is mainly used by community institutions, such as schools and health services, for the preparation of meals for school children, patients and vulnerable groups such as malnourished children and destitutes. In drought years, as might be expected, the number of malnourished children and destitutes increases due to low agricultural production. Consequently, the feeding programme is expanded, and this means that more fuelwood is used for the preparation of meals. In the industrial sector, fuelwood is mainly consumed by bakeries. According to Tietema et al. (1988), one bakery in Dukwe consumed about 85 kg of fuelwood per day. In general, there is a lack of data on the patterns of fuelwood consumption in the non-household sector.

Fuelwood scarcity

In most developing countries, fuelwood scarcity tends to increase around urban centres: concentration of population results in concentrated demand. There are currently two main approaches in assessing the extent of the fuelwood problem, and these are: (a) the gap theory approach; and (b) the method of fuelwood indicators. The former approach, as the name suggests, estimates the gap between fuelwood supply and demand. The supply of fuelwood is normally measured by the increment or yield of fuelwood tree species. The latter approach usually examines indicators associated with fuelwood scarcity, such as increasing labour time, consumption of less preferred species, cutting of live wood, commodification of fuelwood and people's perceptions of the fuelwood problem.

With a few exceptions, the assessment of fuelwood scarcity has not been adequately addressed by surveys in Botswana. The survey undertaken by ERL (1985) is one of the few studies which made an attempt to address the problem comprehensively. Although this study did utilise the indicator approach, it was mainly based on the gap theory approach. Gap theory has many flaws and some scholars contend that it has little value (Munslow et al. 1988; Leach and Mearns 1989). The main flaw is that the gap between supply and demand is not always easy to determine accurately. Also, this approach does not allow for an analysis of the actual social groups affected by the fuelwood problem.

The method of fuelwood scarcity indicators has been utilised by a few surveys in Botswana, although not always in a clear and comprehensive manner. As far as the amount of labour time spent on fuelwood collection is concerned, there is an indication that it is increasing over time in areas near large settlements and urban centres. The amount of time spent on fuelwood collection is, in most cases, directly proportional to the distances to points of fuelwood collection.

Commoditisation of fuelwood has been a common phenomenon in urban areas of Botswana for many years. Although this phenomenon is an indicator of fuelwood scarcity, it can sometimes reflect an increasing division of labour, particularly in urban areas. ERL (1985) revealed that even in relatively small villages of eastern Botswana, such as Goodhope and Masunga, fuelwood was becoming commoditised.

A few surveys also reveal that people tend to harvest less desired species of fuelwood in Botswana. Jelenic and Van Vegten (1983) found that in Matebeleng village, Kgatleng district, people no longer harvested their preferred species of *Combretum*; instead they consumed less desired species of *Acacia Erubescens* and *Dichrostachys Cinerea*. Kgathi (1984) also found that, in some parts of western Kweneng, fuelwood trade had contributed to the depletion of the *Combretum* species.

As far as inferior sources of rural energy are concerned, there is no evidence that their consumption is widespread. Evidence suggests that, in eastern Botswana, cow-dung is mainly burned as a fuel in Goodhope, where commercial agriculture has taken over much of the woodlands. Of the total number of those interviewed, 82 per cent used cow-dung as fuel in Goodhope, and they were mainly poor peasants (ERL 1985).

Fuelwood collection was perceived to be a problem even in relatively smaller villages, like Ditshegwane in Kweneng district, where the points of fuelwood collection were only 5 km from the village (Oki and Majaha-Jartby 1983). The approach of using people's perceptions as an indicator of fuelwood scarcity is very important, because it reveals the views of those who are affected by the problem rather than the views of outsiders. The approach is also useful because it adds a human dimension to the analysis of the fuelwood problem (Leach and Mearns 1989).

Energy programmes and their acceptability to the community

In Botswana, as in other developing countries, an attempt is being made to tackle the fuelwood problem. Three main strategies have been adopted: (1) supply enhancement; (2) substitution; and (3) fuelwood conservation. Fuelwood conservation is attempted by encouraging households to utilise wood-saving stoves. Substitution mainly involves the government encouraging households to switch to coal. Literature on the impact of various energy programmes on supply enhancement is scanty in Botswana, because fuelwood surveys have inadequately addressed this important subject. An attempt will be made, however, to draw evidence from what literature does exist.

One of the few socio-economic surveys which covered aspects of supply enhancement in Botswana revealed that 93 per cent of households in Dukwe saw the need for the establishment of a woodlot around their village. The same survey also revealed that conservation of the woodland resources in Dukwe was seen by the households as a useful strategy. A few households were, however, averse to the idea that the Dukwe authorities should introduce a scheme of the management of woodland resources. They thought such an endeavour by the authorities was not necessary, because they knew how to manage the woodland resources themselves — useful knowledge which the researchers did not attempt to tap.

Conservation of fuelwood was undertaken by the Rural Industries Innovation Centre in the 1970s, and by the Botswana Renewable Technology Project (BRET) in the 1980s. BRET developed new metal stoves which had an efficiency of between 17 and 21 per cent. This was much higher than the efficiency of open fires, estimated to be 9 per cent. High mass stoves tended to have efficiencies even lower than those of open fires in some cases. Although stoves may save fuelwood, it is not certain, in everyday use, that they do so. The testing of stoves in the field needs investigation. Concerning the attitudes of people to stoves the study undertaken by Gay and Zietlow (1985) revealed that more than 60 per cent of the wood-using households in urban centres and large villages had an interest in using the new metal stoves. Another study, in Gakutwe in Kweneng district, revealed that women had an interest in using fuelwood stoves, although their foremost concern was the capital cost associated with the device (Kgathi 1984).

Concerning substitution, it was found that 80 per cent of the wood users in urban centres and large villages of Botswana were in favour of using coal. However, the willingness to use coal was a function of price, in that if the price of coal was half the price of other energy sources, most households would switch to it. If, however, the price of coal was the same as that of other energy sources, the households did not see the need to switch. The willingness to switch to coal was associated with households earning low and middle rather than high and very high incomes (Gay and Zietlow 1985).

Conclusions

This review has revealed flaws in some of the methods adopted by fuelwood researchers in Botswana, the implication being that some of the data collected may not be accurate. The flaws include too much dependence on the questionnaire approach (which should be supplemented by other methods) and lack of supervision of the enumerators.

Using the method of fuelwood scarcity indicators, a number of surveys revealed signs of scarcity in Botswana. However, the indicator approach was not always utilised in a clear and comprehensive manner. There is thus a need for a more thoroughgoing survey of the fuelwood problem in Botswana. Future surveys should endeavour to identify particular social classes affected by the fuelwood problem. It is not sufficient to examine whether or not there is a fuelwood problem; it is also important to indicate whose problem it is.

There is also a need for more surveys to assess the strategies adopted to alleviate the fuelwood problem in Botswana. Although fuelwood stoves are known to conserve fuelwood under laboratory conditions, it is not known whether, in a real life situation, they actually save fuel. Research needs to be undertaken on this important topic. Research is also needed on other strategies for alleviating the fuelwood problem, such as supply enhancement and substitution programmes. The research should also identify other problems which households face, so that an integrated approach to the fuelwood problem can be attempted.

Bibliography

Abel, N.O.J. et al., 1988. *Amelioration of the Soils by Trees: Guidelines for Training in Rapid Appraisal for Agroforestry Research and Extension*, Forestry Commission and Land, Commonwealth Science Council, Harare.

Arntzen, J., 1983. *Firewood Collection in Mosomane*, NIR, University of Botswana, Gaborone.

Energy Resources Limited (ERL), 1985. 'A Study of Energy Utilisation and Requirements in the Rural Sector of Botswana', a report prepared for ODA and the Botswana Ministry of Mineral Resources, ERL, London.

Gay, J. and Zietlow, 1985. 'Botswana Urban Domestic Energy Use and Attitude Survey', Mineral Resources and Water Affairs, Gaborone.

Jelenic, N.E. and Van Vegten, 1983. 'A Pain in the Neck: The Firewood Situation in South Western Kgatleng, Botswana', University of Botswana, Gaborone.

Kgathi, D.L. 1984. 'Firewood Trade Between Rural Kweneng and Urban Gaborone: A Socio-economic Perspective', NIR Working Paper No. 46, University of Botswana, Gaborone.

Leach, G. and Mearns, 1989. *Beyond the Woodfuel Crisis*, Earthscan Publications, London.

Morgan, W.B., 1983. 'Urban Demand: Studying the Commercial Organisation of Woodfuel Supplies' in Woodfuel Surveys, FAO, Rome.

Munslow, B. et al., 1988. *The Fuelwood Trap: A Study of the SADCC Region*, Earthscan Publications, London.

Oki, J. and Majaha-Jartby, 1983. 'Botswana Village Energy Survey Report', BRET and Government of Botswana, Gaborone.

Tietema, T. et al., 1988. 'A Feasibility Study for a Woodland Management and Plantation Scheme', NIR/NORAD, Gaborone.

4 Electricity

4.1 A Case Study of Small Hydro and Grid Extension for Rural Electrification Alternatives and Complementarities

Haile Lul Tebicke and Hailu Gebre Mariam

Rural electrification in Eastern and Southern African Countries (ESAC) has so far been based largely on stand-alone diesel electric generating plant or on the extension of high-voltage transmission grids fed by large hydro and/or thermal electric generating stations. The alternative of furnishing supply at modest investment and competitive cost from a nearby small-hydro plant has rarely been considered in those countries of the sub-region that have ample hydro-power resources.

All countries in the sub-region (except Angola) import petroleum and/or petroleum product supplies, as well as all hardware for electricity supply and utilisation. As a result, in most countries an acute shortage of foreign exchange severely hampers implementation of rural electrification schemes. This should turn attention increasingly to strategies which are less capital-intensive and less dependent on foreign exchange, such as small-hydro plants, where the resource is located near to rural demand. Increasing the local content of small-hydro project implementation has paid off in recent years, considerably reducing costs in a number of Asian and Latin American projects. Local contributions have taken the form of resource assessment at a particular site, design, construction works, and fabrication of relatively simple components of power plant such as hydraulic equipment, low pressure penstocks and gates, as well as simpler types of turbines (e.g., the Banki type). Inadequacy of indigenous technical capacity to make similar local contributions in the ESAC has meant that the few recent small-hydro projects have relied on importing both expertise and equipment. The high costs resulting have frequently fuelled arguments against pursuit of small-hydro projects.

A policy of building and strengthening the requisite range of indigenous technical capacity to substitute substantially for now imported project components could enhance the viability of small-hydro and rural electrification in the ESAC. The case study seeks to elucidate how appropriate small-hydro projects could provide a suitable basis for:

- initiating electric energy supply to a rural community;
- stimulating growth of electricity demand in a rural community for cottage industry, lighting, commercial, basic health and education services to the stage where grid extension becomes economically viable;
- easing the high percentage of foreign exchange required for rural electrification; and
- energy sector technology transfer, adaptation and development in a less developed country.

The case study examines the advantages and drawbacks of small-hydro projects, in contrast with electricity supplies drawn from diesel electric power plants and from large central stations through extensions of high voltage transmission lines.

Site selection

The Jinka area was selected for the case study from four up-country sites that have small-hydro resources and met the basic criteria. Jinka is a market town of 5,000 inhabitants in Ethiopia, about 780 km south of Addis Ababa by road. The nearest town with grid electricity supply is Arba Minch, 265 km north-east of Jinka. There are about 1,980 households in Jinka town and the surrounding four peasant association villages. The villages are typical rural agrarian communities grouped in farmers' co-operatives. The main economic activity is agriculture, and the principal cash crops produced are coffee, cotton and oil seeds.

Energy sample survey

During a visit to Jinka in August 1988, a preliminary survey was conducted into energy use by households, cottage industries, etc. Survey estimates indicate that in the sample households total average monthly energy use amounts to 20.6 megacalories per household. About half of the total is contributed by firewood, 37 per cent by agricultural residues, 9.5 per cent by charcoal, 2.9 per cent by dung and 0.34 per cent by kerosene. Electricity contributes only 0.01 megacalories (or 0.5 per 1,000) of monthly household energy use. A small privately owned diesel electric generating set at present supplies some 2,000 consumers in Jinka town at a flat rate of US $1.75 per bulb per month for 3 hours of supply per night.

Estimates of electric energy needs

As in other similar market towns, electrical energy is obviously needed for coffee decortication, cotton ginning, water pumping, lighting, refrigeration, flour milling, educational and health purposes. The contribution of electricity to national energy use is put at 1.3 per cent of the total in CESEN's comprehensive study (September 1986) of the energy sector in Ethiopia. This ratio was applied to estimate the initial electric energy kwh and kw power levels when utility supply is established, using a 50 per cent plant factor. Corresponding load and energy demand growths were projected for the study area, by standard methods.

Alternative sources of energy

Small-hydro plants

On the basis of available maps, a small-hydro site about 25 km from Jinka town had been identified on the middle reaches of the Neri River before its confluence with the Maki, a tributary of the Omo. A reconnaissance field trip to the site confirmed a 1.5 km stretch of cataract that would facilitate the inexpensive harnessing of the hydro-energy. The approximate locations of the diversion weir, headrace channel route, head pond and power house were determined. Approximate head development was estimated from contour maps and water availability assessed from the flow duration curve of the Neri River. Preliminary design of the relevant structures suggested that a small-hydro plant with an installed capacity of 600 kw would cost Birr 2.89 million (US$1.45m).

Grid extension

The 132 kv line from Arba Minch, 225 km long, would have 40 mva minimum power capacity. It would be a single circuit line on galvanised steel towers (300 m span) and have a 132/66 kv sub-station at Konso and one of 132/15 kv at Jinka. Applying unit costs of high voltage transmission lines under construction in Ethiopia in 1988, total investment required for the grid extension was estimated to be Birr 34.15 million (US$17.10m).

Diesel

The third alternative, a diesel-powered plant on the outskirts of Jinka town, would have two generating sets each rated 300 kw including generation and distribution panels (2 x 800 kva), 0.4/15 kv in-door transformers, etc. A fuel storage tank, minimum building requirements and site works were also included in the estimated cost of Birr 1.60 million (US$0.80m).

Investment and energy costs

Cost estimates were arrived at for the three alternative schemes, using 1988 unit costs obtained from the Ethiopian Electric Authority (EELPA) and from the Chinese team surveying small-hydro resources for the Ministry of Agriculture, etc. Economic analysis of project costs for each alternative predicted the kw and kwh costs. Operation costs in each case were estimated on the basis of current EELPA cost figures. Maintenance costs for hydro-plant and grid extension are taken to be 1.5 and 1 per cent of the annualised costs respectively. Annual diesel plant maintenance cost is estimated at 15 per cent of investment. Fuel costs are computed additionally. The cost of furnishing grid supply excludes the investment in the proportionate part of central station generation capacity. Examination of investments and supply costs of shorter grid extensions indicates that grid extension and small-hydro kwh costs become comparable only for extensions of 25—30 km or less.

Main findings

The case study shows that supplying electricity to Jinka and the rural communities in its environs from the small-hydro site 25 km away on the Neri River would be the least-cost option in annualised foreign exchange costs (Fig. 1) at any time in the project cycle, in comparison with the diesel plant and the grid extension.

Figure 1. Cumulative annualised foreign exchange costs of alternative electricity supply for Jinka area.

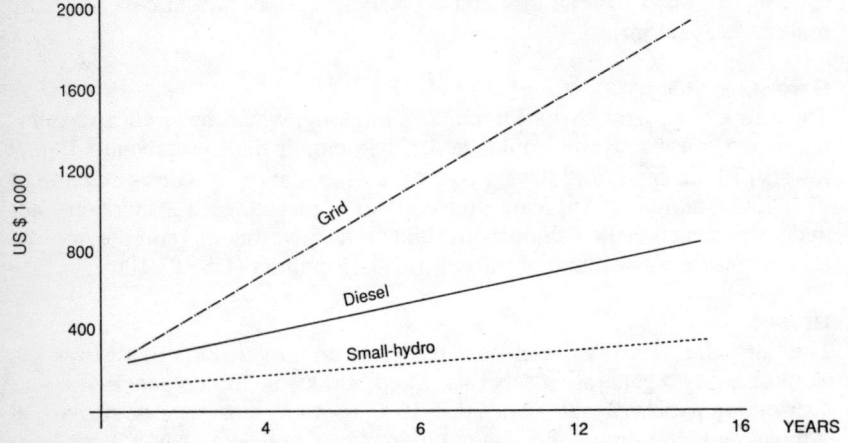

The small-hydro plant would furnish energy at about one tenth and one third of the cost per kwh of grid extension and diesel electric supply respectively (Fig. 2a). It would also have the least maintenance cost, only one tenth of grid extension and less than four per cent of the diesel plant (Fig. 2b).

The diesel project has the lowest overall first investment cost, about half that of the small-hydro plant and just under four per cent of the grid extension cost respectively (Fig. 2c). The diesel project also has the lowest annualised investment cost (Fig. 2d). This is the usual justification for decisions to install diesel plants. But note that the engine, at least, would have to be replaced after the fifteenth year of service as it would be worn out and unserviceable by then.

Operating costs are least for the grid extension, being 71 per cent of small-hydro plant and 3.5 per cent of diesel operating costs (Fig. 2e). Note, however, that except for modest costs of manpower, the operating expenses of the diesel plant must be met mainly in foreign exchange for fuel, lubricants and spare parts. The operating costs of grid-extension also have a high

Figure 2. Comparative costs of alternative electricity supply sources for Jinka

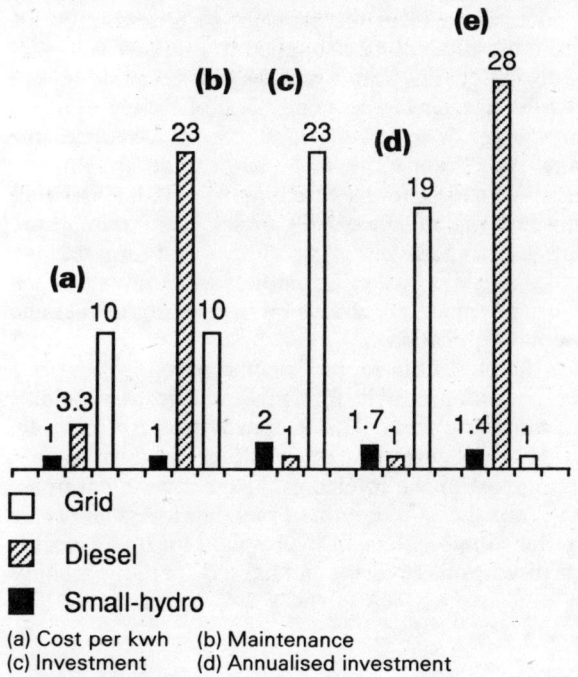

☐ Grid
▨ Diesel
■ Small-hydro

(a) Cost per kwh (b) Maintenance
(c) Investment (d) Annualised investment
(e) operating costs

foreign exchange component for amortisation of the high foreign exchange investment and for imported spare parts.

The small-hydro plant is likely to attain a high load factor within a few years of project completion. The equivalent diesel plant offers the same advantage. The grid extension has the capacity to deliver up to 30 mw. Its load factor would therefore remain very low unless industrial and/or mining ventures with a high electricity demand are established in the Jinka area.

Conclusions

The following are some of the features which make small-hydro electricity supply particularly attractive for small towns and rural communities where the hydro-resource is available nearby.

1. Lower overall foreign exchange requirement than alternatives during the service life of the project. As recently demonstrated in other developing regions, small hydro offers opportunities for indigenous capacity to design

and engineer small-hydro projects, as well as to furnish, at competitive cost, less sophisticated elements of hydro-plant such as hydraulic gates, low-pressure penstocks, draft tubes, simpler turbines (e.g., the Banki type). This lower foreign exchange intensity relieves the pressure to generate foreign exchange earnings from the use of electricity supplied to rural areas.

2. The lower cost of producing energy from a small-hydro resource lessens the need to set high tariffs to recover the economic cost of supply — as for diesel or grid extension sources. The lower production cost reduces the burden of subsidies, if any. And lower tariffs facilitate demand growth.

3. Small-hydro plants require modest levels of operating and maintenance skills. The high operating and maintenance skills diesel plants require are notoriously difficult to attract to, and retain in, small town and rural settings. Lack of adequate levels of such skills further jeopardises continuity of diesel-based electricity supply, usually made precarious by irregularity of fuel and lubricant supplies to up-country locations.

4. Substitution of grid for diesel electric supply is commonly regarded as a strategy that reduces the operating cost in foreign exchange of providing electricity to small towns and rural areas. This is usually true for recurrent operating costs. Substituting grid for diesel supply would be disadvantageous, however, if the amortisation cost of the foreign exchange investment in the grid extension exceeds the annual cost of imported fuel, lubricants and spare parts for the diesel plant. Substitution of small-hydro plant for diesel electric supply is free from such disadvantage, as the annualised foreign exchange cost of the hydro-power is low.

Recommendations

The case study clearly indicates that where the resource is available near the locality, small-hydro electricity supply offers considerable advantages over both grid extension and diesel electric sources, for a rural electrification scheme. Small hydro offers considerable scope for indigenous technical capacity to contribute to reducing investment and supply costs, especially in foreign exchange. Commensurate local content contributions and savings cannot be expected from the alternatives because of the high level of technical sophistication of the diesel and grid equipment components involved. We hope that the present case study will encourage similar case studies in other countries in the sub-region endowed with small-hydro resources. It is recommended that in such countries studies be conducted into policies that would vigorously encourage the growth of the full range of indigenous technical capacity needed for wide-scale development of small-hydro resources.

References

Cesen, 1986. 'Energy Survey in Ethiopia: Main Report and Technical Report 2 on Hydro Resources'.

Commission of the European Community's Directorate-General for Development, 1985. 'Rural Electrification in the Developing Countries'.

Ethiopian Ministry of Agriculture, 1988. 'Small-Hydro Resources Survey' by Chinese team.

Ethiopian Ministry of Water Resources and Electric Power, 1986. 'Small-Hydro Power Development in China'.

IDRC, 1986. 'Household Energy Consumption in Rio de Janiero Shanty Towns'.

Haile Lul Tebicke and Hailu G. Mariam. 'Small-Hydro and/or Grid Extension for Rural Electrification Alternatives and Complementarities'. SAREC-IDRC sponsored energy research project.

Ministry of Supply and Services, Canada, 1987. 'A User's Guide to Reducing the Costs of Operating Diesel Power Plants under 500 kw'.

Ontario Ministry of Energy, 1988. 'Small Hydro Developers Course'.

4.2 Energy Demand and Consumption Patterns of Maseru Peri-urban Areas, with Particular Reference to Low-income Locations

L.M. Khalema

Lesotho, like most developing countries in Eastern and Southern Africa which are dependent on imported oil, has grave problems in several areas, amongst which are both the modern and the traditional energy sectors. Since energy is an integral part of the national economy, its inadequacy and occasional unavailability severely disrupt virtually every section of the economy.

Some attention has been focused on the energy problems of the peri-urban areas where resources such as dung, fuelwood and agricultural residues are depleted more rapidly than they can be replenished, but no national energy policy, including concrete investment decisions, has been formulated to meet the needs of the sector. Another problem is lack of local data on domestic energy demand and consumption.

This study was aimed at identifying actions and strategies which could help improve the situation by identifying specific needs and existing problems. It is an attempt to lay the basis for building up a national picture of energy consumption patterns. The study set out to analyse energy demand and energy use in the household sector of the five peri-urban low-income areas of Maseru (the capital) which received a government subsidy towards reticulation and electrification. It involved a survey of electrified and non-electrified households in each of the selected areas, a total of 200 households. The main objective was to investigate why power demand in Lesotho remained 'suppressed', in spite of the government subsidy.

Lesotho is almost entirely supplied with electricity from the Electricity Supply Commission of South Africa (ESCOM). Only about 2 per cent of the total population (estimated to be over 1.5 million by the 1986 population census) use electricity. The situation has changed recently following the commissioning in November 1988 and March 1989 of 210 kw and 2 mw mini-hydro plants in Semonkong and Mantsonyane respectively. The sites of both plants are in the central mountainous area of Lesotho.

The long history of electricity in Lesotho — five decades — makes it remarkable that the percentage of population having access to electricity should be so low. The causes of this phenomenon require understanding and correction if the level of electricity consumption and overall living standards in the country are to be raised.

Energy research and national policy

According to the conclusion of the Third Five Year Development Plan (1980—85), Lesotho aimed at reducing its dependence on South Africa for electricity. Simultaneously, the plan foresaw the extension of electricity reticulation in the peri-urban areas of Maseru, district towns and rural areas. The two mini-hydro plants, and another two envisaged to come on line later in 1989, are in accordance with the above conclusion. It is essential that energy demand and consumption patterns be studied and understood if this objective is to be pursued and an appropriate energy policy followed which would contribute to solving some of the economic problems facing the country.

Lesotho's economic base is dependent on the South African mines: no less than 50 per cent of the economically active male population get their income from there. Their earnings constitute 42 per cent of the Gross National Product. Prospects for agricultural production to make a major contribution to foreign exchange earnings are limited by the country's small size and mountainous terrain which leaves only about 13 per cent of land area suitable for crop production. This is the background against which energy research must make its contribution to national policy.

The research programme

Research combined the following elements:
- compilation of statistics on number of consumers and energy consumption growth, per monthly bills at the start of reticulation as compared with forecast at the start of the projects;
- a house to house energy demand survey of the selected five peri-urban areas;
- gathering of technical information relating to construction of the supply system in the selected areas;
- making suggestions regarding reasonable and affordable electrifiable structures (assumptions pertinent to cost required for renovation of existing structures were made by visual inspection).

The methodology used was to choose typical peri-urban housing settlements, to some degree accessible, and to target families with low to middle incomes (i.e. households with a total monthly income under M400 in the case of Khubetsoana, and under M650 elsewhere). All the selected areas have prospects for development of small-scale industries: Khubetsoana, Tsenola, Tsosane, Lower Seoli and Maseru East. In May 1988 a house-to-house survey was carried out. Preliminary investigations aimed to determine:

- present electricity consumption vis-à-vis requirements;
- availability, quantity and cost of existing (small-scale) electrical appliances and likelihood of acquiring more;

66 Electricity

- possible increase of usage of electricity depending on tariffs;
- examination of methods of heating, cooking and lighting, etc.
- potential consumers' ability to pay for the service when available.

It was hypothesised that rural migration to the peri-urban areas studied was with the intent to benefit from improved and electrified housing; that prospective consumers had their houses wired and had acquired appliances which operate on gas and electricity; that residents prioritise their needs and perspectives; that there was fuel consumption. These hypotheses were tested.

Table 1
Maseru peri-urban electrification programme

Reticulation of	Duration	No. of plots	1986[1] population	1988 present consumers	Connection fee (Maloti)[2]
Khubetsoana (LIH)	Zone A 1985–			Zone A 48	
	Zone B 1988–	865	5785	Zone B —	580.00
Tsenola	1987–	—	3697	115	1645.00
Tsosane	1987–	—	3028	45	1272.00
Lower Seoli	1986–	—	794	50	2338.00
Maseru East	1986–	—	1118	66	1426.00

1. Some of the areas have undergone rapid development since 1986, e.g. Lower Seoli.
2. 1 Loti = 1 South African Rand = (+ US$0.43), November 1988.

In carrying out calculations the following figures were applied:
- average unit price (c/kwh) for all tariff sales 1988/89 from Lesotho Electricity Commission (LEC) (budget price): 15.40 c/kwh;
- purchase of power from ESCOM is calculated from bulk monthly tariff: 16.97 R/kw max./3.066 c/kw and these estimates:
- LEC load factor 42 per cent;
- transmission and distribution losses 15 per cent;
- unit average price for purchase of power:

$$\left(\frac{16.97 \times 100 \times 12 + 3.066}{8{,}760 \times 0.42} \right) \times 1.15^+$$

+ Correction for losses between the intake point and low tension line at the consumers' point.

Basis for estimation
(1) Lifetime for the low tension (LT) high tension (HT) distribution system = 20 years.
(2) Discount rate (real rate of interest) = 6 per cent.
    Annuity factor = .087185
(3) Annual maintenance and operation costs of investment = 5 per cent

Table 2
Summary cost estimates for reticulation of the peri-urban areas

Area	Investment	Maloti Annual capital cost	Annual operation & maint. cost	Estimated gross revenue / c/kwh for all sales[1]
1) Tsosane	125,807	10,968	6,290	2.36
2) Lower Seoli	116,896	10,192	5,845	2.90
3) Khubetsoana	125,943	10,980	6,297	0.95
4) Tsenola	267,233	23,299	13,362	-25.22
5) Maseru East	141,401	12,328	7,070	2.12

1. Gross revenue to cover *all other costs* (i.e. administration buildings, transport, personnel) excluding capital costs, operation and maintenance costs and purchase of power. According to the LEC budget all other costs amount to 15—20 per cent of the total budget sum. In other words, of the average unit tariff sale of 15.40 c/kwh, 3 c/kwh goes to cover the above-mentioned *all other costs*. However, results in the last column above show that not one of the five peri-urban areas contribute positively to the financial position of the LEC.

Summary and conclusions

It was established on the whole that residents of the selected areas are enthusiastic about development, and more specifically electrification, in their areas. However, the question still remains as to why power demand in Lesotho is 'suppressed'. Reasons could be:

- the ever-rising cost of electricity;
- periodic tariff increases by the bulk electricity supplier (ESCOM) leading to commensurate adjustments by the LEC on their consumer tariffs;
- high cost of internal wiring of houses; and
- lack of established guidelines for new connection, leading to irregularly high connection fees.

The following recommendations are put forward with a view to aiding policy-makers in future cost-effective electrification programmes in the peri-urban areas.

1. Intensification of marketing techniques by the LEC and dissemination of information about electricity to enable beneficiaries to evaluate the advantages of being connected, leading to a rise in demand for electricity and economically self-supporting electrification schemes over time.

2. LEC should fix tariffs in such a way that consumers' decisions about consumption result in an efficient use of the country's energy resources and institute a fixed, affordable connection fee that is simple to administer and easy for the consumer to understand. The capital outlay would then be recovered through consumers' future consumption.

3. LEC should continue to have the right to govern consumption, through its appropriate tariff, and develop the network on a sound economic basis. However, in case(s) of an exception from LEC's network development

programme, the prospective consumer should finance the entire project.

4. For future comprehensive planning and economic utilisation of funds, duration of construction projects is a critical factor and should always be predefined.

5. The (in part political) decision that certain areas should have access to electricity may incur present and future expenses which were not provided for through either power sales or government's allotted investment subsidy. It could lead to subsidisation of new consumers by the existing ones in order to cover the distribution costs. A complete analysis of these costs needs to be done prior to undertaking projects. While subsidisation of one consumer by another is not necessarily wrong it must fall within a defined policy. In our case, a defined policy that an extra cent is charged for every kwh sold and then diverted to an electrification fund, could suffice.

6. The existing Development Committees in the targeted areas should set up a 'Suspense Account' for the peri-urban inhabitants and use this to ensure preparedness and timely payment for an electricity connection during reticulation.

7. Set up a revolving fund that will facilitate an affordable connection fee and the implementation of a system of deferred payment without further hurting the financial position of the LEC.

8. In planned areas like Khubetsoana, incorporate wiring of the houses, carried out by a contracted company, into the Housing Corporation project's loan.

9. Adherence to the criteria determining qualification for the government subsidy is essential.

10. Intensification and improvement of the energy conservation campaign through the media.

4.3 Opportunities and Prospects for Energy Conservation in the Tanzania Electric Supply Company Limited

M.L. Luhanga
(in collaboration with B.E. Luhanga)

Electric power plays an indispensable catalytic role in economic and social development and in industrialisation. In recognition of this fact, the government of Tanzania has, through the Tanzania Electric Supply Company (TANESCO), placed a high priority on the efficient operation and further development of the country's electricity generation, transmission and distribution facilities.

An electricity generation facility transforms one form of energy into another form of energy. In a hydro-electric system, the potential energy of water stored in a dam is transformed into electrical energy, whereas in an oil thermal power plant chemical energy embodied in the petroleum fuel is converted into electric energy. We shall discuss this energy flow through a generation system in a little more detail later.

Energy conservation in TANESCO's thermal systems

In an electric utility, energy conservation opportunities exist in the generation, transmission, distribution and end-use areas. Energy conservation opportunities related to electricity end-uses are not directly under the control of TANESCO and they do not form part of this report. We confine ourselves to a discussion of energy conservation opportunities in the generation, transmission and distribution of electricity by TANESCO. And since a parallel report is looking at energy conservation opportunities in hydro-plants, we further confine ourselves to a discussion of energy conservation opportunities in TANESCO's isolated thermal systems.

In Appendix A (p. 73) we present statistics on the fuel consumption of TANESCO's isolated thermal generation systems for the year 1980.

In computing the conversion efficiencies at each station, the energy conservation factors used were those set out in the following table.

Table 1
Energy conservation efficiencies

Fuel type	Conversion efficiency	
	kcal/tonne (x 10^6)	gj/tonne
Gas oil	10.2	42.7
Furnace oil	9.6–9.9	40.2–41.5

Electricity

For electricity we use a conversion factor of 860 kcal/kwh which is equivalent to 3.6 gj/kwh.

In order to account for evaporation of fuel from oil storage tanks, leakage from power station fuel delivery pipes, and possible gas oil usage in trucks, we have made allowances of 1 per cent, 5 per cent and 15 per cent of consumption to account for these losses.

Appendix A indicates that there is considerable room for improving the thermal conversion efficiency of TANESCO's thermal generation units. The manufacturer's own recommendation is a conversion efficiency of the order of 38 per cent, which is a figure much higher than conversion efficiencies that have been achieved by TANESCO. To convey the magnitude of the problem we cite historical data on conversion efficiency at Singida, where a new generating station (with 2 x 640 kw sets) was commissioned, and the old power station abandoned in 1983.

Table 2
Conversion efficiencies at Singida

Year	Conversion efficiency	Conversion efficiency with 20% allowances for fuel losses
1980	24.13	30.17
1981	22.15	27.81
1982	23.87	29.83
1983	23.00	28.75
1984	40.44	50.56
1985	38.65	48.32
1986	32.85	41.07
1987	12.30	15.38

One notices that from 1984 (the first full year of operation of the new power station) efficiency was within the order of magnitude suggested by the manufacturer. Efficiency dropped steadily, however, until by 1987 it was less than 50 per cent of the manufacturer's suggested figure — even with a very generous 20 per cent allowance for fuel losses!

In general, there are two technical solutions to energy conservation: (a) elimination or reduction of energy losses in existing technologies; and (b) replacement of existing devices with more energy-efficient ones. Objectives, orders of priority and technical solutions to conservation in generation, transmission and distribution systems are covered elsewhere and will not be repeated here (Ministry of Water et al., 1985; M.L. and B.E. Luhanga, 1988).

Financial and economic analysis of conservation options

Financial and economic evaluation has to proceed by comparing the

profitability of implementing the following three energy conservation measures:
(a) improvement of operational and maintenance strategies; (b) rehabilitation of existing systems; and (c) installation of new equipment. The comparisons are made by assuming each of the measures above is implemented to yield the same heat rate for a machine of a given capacity.

Two types of profitability evaluation are to be carried out — a financial evaluation and an economic evaluation. The financial evaluation is carried out using current official market prices for costs, applying the official exchange rate for conversion of costs in foreign currency, and giving due consideration to all taxes and duties. The result of this analysis will indicate which of the three options given above is most profitable to the user, TANESCO. Detailed formulas for carrying out this evaluation are shown in Appendix B.

An economic evaluation is carried out with costs and exchange rates adjusted to reflect 'economic efficiency prices' of the inputs. Also, taxes and duties are not considered. The results of such an analysis will indicate which of the three options given above is the most profitable to the nation, Tanzania. Detailed formulas for carrying out the economic evaluation are also given in Appendix B.

In both the economic and the financial analysis, the time value of money is considered by using a real interest rate which is taken to be approximately equal to the difference between the nominal bank interest rate and the inflation rate.

Comparisons are made between a baseline case involving operating the present thermal systems in their present condition (i.e., business as usual) and the three alternatives. Comparisons can be made on the basis of:
(a) an annual worth method of discounted cash flow analysis;
(b) the annual saving in foreign currency;
(c) the undiscounted payback period for foreign currency;
(d) the discounted payback period for foreign currency.
Formulas are given in Appendix B for computing all these indices.

Conclusion

Energy conservation opportunities in TANESCO's thermal system have been discussed and a framework for the financial and economic evaluation of various alternatives to energy conservation has been developed. It has not yet been possible, however, to apply the framework to TANESCO's system and obtain numerical results.

References

Luhanga, M.L. and B.E. Luhanga. 1988. 'Opportunities and Prospects of Conservation in TANESCO', unpublished report.

Ministry of Water, Energy and Minerals. June 1985. *Consultancy Report on TANESCO's Financial Position and Outlook*, Dar es Salaam.

Acknowledgement

The authors acknowledge with gratitude financial support from SAREC and from IDRC. The authors also acknowledge the support of the University of Dar es Salaam (for Prof. M.L. Luhanga) and the Tanzania Electric Supply Company Limited (TANESCO) for providing time and facilities in support of the research on which results reported here are based. The authors are also indebted to Miss Grace Chamshama who did the typing.

Energy Conservation in the Tanzania Electric Supply Company Limited 73

Appendix A
Thermal generation efficiencies in isolated systems 1980

Generating station	Units generated (kwh)	Fuel consumed (tonnes)	Station heat rate (g/kwh)	Efficiency (%)	Efficiency less 1% losses (%)	Efficiency less 51% losses (%)	Efficiency less 15% losses (%)
Mafia	658,402.0	290.7	441.6	20.29	20.49	21.36	23.87
Arusha	1,673,330.0	713.0	426.1	21.02	21.24	22.13	24.73
Chamwino	61,268.0	—	—	—	—	—	—
Dodoma	8,042,908.0	2,248.6	279.6	32.04	32.37	33.73	37.70
Mpwapwa	699,356.0	245.0	350.3	25.57	25.83	26.92	30.09
Ubungo	9,413,380.0	2,635.0	279.9	32.00	32.33	33.69	37.65
Iringa	652,190.0	282.2	432.8	20.70	20.91	21.79	24.35
Bukoba	5,369,824.0	1,823.2	339.5	26.38	26.65	27.77	31.04
Kigoma	3,246,491.0	1,090.7	336.0	26.66	26.93	28.07	31.37
Kilwa Masoko	62,090.0	55.4	892.4	10.04	10.14	10.57	11.81
Lindi	70,740.0	31.6	446.7	20.05	20.26	21.11	23.59
Nachingwea	1,020,120.0	331.9	325.4	27.53	27.81	28.98	32.39
Kiabakari	1,020,556.0	355.8	348.7	25.69	25.95	27.04	30.23
Musoma	8,691,582.0	2,390.0	275.0	32.58	32.91	34.29	38.33
Mbeya	3,488,807.0	1,364.3	391.1	22.91	23.14	24.11	26.95
Tukuyu	3,602,190.0	923.7	256.4	34.94	35.29	36.77	41.10
Tunduma	17,280.0	14.7	850.1	10.54	10.64	11.09	12.40
Mtwara	4,288,718.0	1,681.4	392.0	22.85	23.08	24.05	26.88
Mwanza	43,749,736.0	10,871.1	248.5	36.05	36.42	37.95	42.41
Sumbawanga	53,630.0	31.6	588.5	15.22	15.38	16.02	17.91
Songea	2,008.537.0	680.3	338.7	26.45	26.72	27.84	31.12
Shinyanga	3,698,553.0	984.1	266.1	33.67	34.01	35.44	39.61
Singida	1,686,309.0	625.9	371.2	24.13	24.38	25.41	28.39
Tabora	4,619,220.0	1,584.0	342.9	26.12	26.39	27.50	30.73
Total	107,895,217.0	31,254.2	289.7	30.93	31.24	32.55	36.38

Appendix B
Economic and financial analysis

Options

The efficiency of transformation of an existing thermal power station may be ancreased by improving operation and maintenance procedures, rehabilitating the plant, or replacing it with a new one. The economic and financial implications of these three options are usually quite different and one is faced with the problem of deciding which option to implement. Taking the continued operation of the power plant as a baseline case, a decision can be reached by comparing the annual economic and financial costs of the three options to the corresponding costs of the existing thermal plant. Below we present an analytical framework for carrying out this analysis.

Definitions

Let
- Q = Total annual production of energy by a thermal plant
- t = Annual plant operating time in hours
- pr = Plant rated power output in kw
- n = Plant economic lifetime in years
- a_e = Economic capital recovery factor
- a_f = Financial capital recovery factor
- i = Economic interest rate
- j = Financial interest rate
- X = Exchange rate (Tanzanian shillings to one US $)
- Y = Load factor
- S_x = Shadow factor of foreign exchange
- C_d = Specific economic investment cost in foreign currency in US $ per kw
- C_t = Specific economic investment cost in local currency in Tanzanian shillings per kw
- f_c = Fraction of C_t that is in foreign currency
- T = Total economic capital investment in Tanzanian shillings
- T_1 = Import tax on plant and equipment as a proportion of capital cost C_d
- C_p = Untaxed price of fuel in Tanzanian shillings/kg
- f_p = Fraction of C_p that is in foreign currency
- T_{pe} = Tax on fuel in Tanzanian shillings/kg
- C_{pe} = Fuel cost with shadow factoring of foreign exchange
- C_{cp} = Annual economic capital cost in Tanzanian shillings
- C_{pp} = Annual economic cost for fuel
- b_p = Specific consumption of fuel (kg/kwh)
- C_1 = Cost for unskilled labour
- S_1 = Shadow factor for unskilled labour

Energy Conservation in the Tanzania Electric Supply Company Limited

C_{tr} = Transport cost for fuel (Tshs/kg)
f_t = Fraction of C_{tr} that is in foreign currency
b_m = Unskilled labourers required for full-time operation
C_{10} = Annual economic labour cost
L_b = Specific lubricant consumption (kg/kwh)
C_{1u} = Lubricant cost (TShs/kg)
f_{1u} = Fraction of C_{1u} that is in foreign currency
C_a = Annual economic lubricant cost
C = Total annual economic cost
M_s = Service cost factor in fraction of capital cost (C_d) per hour of operation
M_t = Service cost factor in local currency (including costs of skilled labour) as a fraction of capital cost (C_t) per hour of operation
f_m = Fraction of M_t that is in foreign currency
C_m = Annual economic maintenance and service cost
T_f = Financial capital investment
C_f = Financial cost for fuel
C_{fa} = Annual financial cost for fuel
T_{fa} = Annual financial capital cost
T_{10} = Annual financial labour cost
F_{1a} = Annual financial lubricant cost
F_m = Annual financial maintenance and service costs
F = Total annual financial costs

Formulas

Load Factor, Y
$Y = Q/(P_r * t)$

Economic analysis

(a) Economic capital recovery factor, a_e
$a_e = (i*(1+i)^n)/((1+i)^6 n - 1)$

(b) Total investment costs ($T*n_m$), T
$T = P_r * \{C_d * S_x * X + C_i (1 - f_c) + C_t * S_x * f_c\}$?

(c) Economic fuel cost, C_{pe}
$C_{pe} = C_p(1-f_p) + C_p*S_x*f_p + C_{tr}(1-f_t(+C_{tr}*S_x*f_t$

(d) Annual economic capital cost, C_{cp}
$C_{cp} = P_r*a_e*\{C_d*S_x*X + C_t(1-f_c) + C_t*S_x*f_c\}$?

(e) Annual economic fuel cost, C_{pp}
$C_{pp} = P_r*t*Y*b_p*C_{pe}$

(f) Annual economic unskilled labour cost, C_{10}
$C_{10} = C_1*S_1*t*b_m$

(g) Annual economic lubricant cost, C_{1a}
$C_{1a} = P_r*t*Y*1_b*\{C1u(1-f_{1u}) + C_{1u}*S_x*F_{1u}\}$?

(h) Annual economic maintenance and service cost, C_m
$C_m = P_r*t*\{M_s*C_d*X*S_x + M_t*C_t*(1-f_m) + M_t*C_t*S_x*f_c\}$?

(i) Total annual economic cost, C
$$C = C_{cp} + C_{pp} + C_{10} + C_{1a} + C_m$$

Financial analysis

(a) Financial capital recovery factor, a_f
$$a_f = (j*(1+j)^6 n)/((1+j)^6 n - 1)$$
(b) Financial capital investment, T_f
$$T_f = P_r * \{C_d * X * (1+T_1) + C_t?$$
(c) Financial cost of fuel, C_f
$$C_f = C_p + T_{pe}$$
(d) Annual financial capital cost, T_{fa}
$$T_{fa} = P_r * a_f * \{C_d * X * (1+T_1) + C_t?$$
(e) Annual financial fuel cost, C_{fa}
$$C_{fa} = P_r * t * Y * b_p * C_f$$
(f) Annual financial labour cost, F_{10}
$$F_{10} = C_1 * t * b_m$$
(g) Annual financial lubricant cost, F_{1a}
$$F_{1a} = P_r * t * Y * L_b * C_{1u}$$
(h) Annual financial maintenance and service cost, F_m
$$F_m = P_r * t * \{M_s * C_d * (1+T_1) + M_t * C_t?$$
(i) Total annual financial cost, F
$$F = T_{fa} + C_{fa} + F_{10} + F_{1a} + F_m$$

Comparisons

(a) The annual savings in foreign exchange in comparison with the baseline case will be given by the formula below where the extra subscripts 'base' and 'alt' refer to the baseline and alternative options, respectively:
$$F_{save} = Q/X * \{[(b_p)_{base} - (b_p)_{alt}] * C_p * f_p + [(L_b)_{base} - (L_b)_{alt}]$$
$$* C_{1u} * f_{1u} + P_r * t * [(M_s * C_d)_{base} - (m_s * C_d)_{alt}]?$$
where F_{save} is the foreign currency saving.
(b) The undiscounted payback period for foreign currency, T_a, is given by:
$$T_a = \{P_r * [(C_d)_{base} - (C_d)_{alt}]?/F_{save}$$
(c) The discounted payback period for foreign currency, T_b, is given by:
$$T_b = \{\ln[1/(1 - i/T_a)]?/\{\ln(1+i)?$$

4.4 Opportunities and Prospects for Energy Conservation in an Electrical Utility: a Zambian Case

Abel Mbewe

In a developing country like Zambia, power demand can increase rapidly. To meet the demand, heavy investments are required in the electric power sector. In addition to this capital outlay, long lead times are required to implement power schemes. Conservation offers a means of reducing the gap between demand and supply which is likely to grow in coming years. The energy saved could be used to supply part of the demand and relieve the immediate pressure to commit scarce resources to develop new sources of energy.

In Zambia about 93 per cent of the units generated by Zambia Electricity Supply Corporation Limited (ZESCO) come from hydro-power plants. The losses in ZESCO networks are about 13 per cent. Experience shows that ZESCO is not being operated at the high level of efficiency that can be achieved. Hitherto no studies have been undertaken to explore ways of lowering losses. The present study established the following objectives:

1. To compare the average losses in ZESCO with those in utilities of developed countries sustaining losses of around 10 per cent.
2. To look into the technical and economic possibilities of lowering the losses in ZESCO's generation, transmission, distribution and supply networks.
3. To explore ways of quantifying theft of power in ZESCO networks and look into the technological solution to this problem.

The methodology adopted to pursue these objectives involved the following:
1. Data collection in the form of an energy audit at each stage, starting with primary inputs to generation (e.g., water) and ending with sales in physical units.
2. Technical analysis of opportunities to achieve savings at each stage, based on the application of standard engineering approaches.
3. Rough estimation of monetary cost to implement savings of a megawatt or megawatt-hour as appropriate.
4. Development of a method to identify theft.
5. Use of the above method to determine losses and to suggest technical means to reduce them.

Technical opportunities for conservation in generation

ZESCO has three major hydro-power stations. Kafue Gorge Power Station was chosen because it is the largest. There are six generating sets of 150 mw capacity each. The yearly average operating time for each machine is approximately 6,400 hours.

The losses in the turbines average 10 per cent. The highest efficiency that can be obtained on Kafue Gorge turbines is 95 per cent: the losses due to reduction in efficiency are thus 5 per cent. At full load this accounts for 7.5 mw with a generation cost of KO.01616 per kwh, yielding a financial loss of K2908.80 per day. The turbines have an average yearly operation time of approximately 6,400 hours, so that the annual financial loss per turbine would be K775,680, and the total annual loss for all turbines K4,654,080 (approximately US$455,000 at late 1988 exchange rates).

Transmission and distribution losses

Conservation of energy for utilities such as ZESCO is a very important parameter. Because of excess capacity in generation plant, and since the primary input to generation is water, ZESCO has had no great financial incentive to reduce losses. Energy conservation opportunities for such organisations are numerous though not all of them can be effected: losses of energy in some areas cannot be avoided, but can be reduced.

The losses in ZESCO can be classified in two categories: technical losses and non-technical losses.

Technical losses
These result from transmission line and transformer losses. Energy conservation opportunities to counter technical losses are careful selection of transformers to be used so as to minimise the load losses, I^2R, hysteresis and eddy currents.

Non-technical losses
There are two main classes of non-technical losses in the system. One class encompasses operational deficiencies in the system; the other results from thefts by consumers.

Operational deficiencies: A number of operational deficiencies contribute to non-technical losses. A survey of 100 households in various townships of Lusaka during this project shows that losses due to metering include fixed charge assessment and inadequate recording of electricity consumption.

Some domestic consumers are direct-connected because single-phase meters are unavailable. The fixed charge units are assessed as follows:

Fixed charge units = total load × load factor × no. of hours

The total load is the sum of the loads of all lighting points, sockets, geysers and other appliances in the house.

After meters were installed in some townships of Lusaka, comparisons between the fixed charge assessment and the meter readings for three consecutive months were made. Results showed that 12 per cent of households consumed on average more electricity than the estimated consumption.

Improper recording of electricity consumption was observed in 48 per cent of households, where the number of units of electricity consumed each month was said to be constant — an obviously unreliable result.

Theft of power: Theft of power is the illegal consumption of electricity. Household consumers are the main culprits in this practice. Theft stratagems include damaging of meters by increasing friction on the disc bearing, rendering readings inaccurate; re-wiring so as to bypass the meter; and replacing of main circuit breakers with those of higher rating in order to draw more current than the limit.

Checks on meters suspected of registering inaccurate readings have shown various methods of *tampering with the meter*. In most cases the meter is physically damaged and hardly records at all. A possible solution to this problem would be to put the meter in an enclosure and seal it so that the consumer has no access to it. The current exercise of replacing Lusaka's old and damaged meters has partly solved this problem. Meters are put in one enclosure which is locked, and the key is kept by a caretaker. This idea of grouping all meters in one enclosure is most suitable in flats.

When a disconnection is effected, some consumers re-connect the supply and *bypass the meter*. In some of these cases, the illegal wiring is done at night and removed in the morning, so that during the day — when ZESCO patrols take place — the supply remains disconnected. A possible solution would be to disconnect the supply from the pole.

Some consumers who are on fixed charge assessment *remove the main circuit breakers* and replace these with those of a higher rating in order to draw more current than their limit. This practice is very common in peri-urban areas. These illegal consumers extend their buildings and supply power to these extensions. Some of them instal welding machines in their backyards, others supply power to their neighbours at a fee. The only solution to this problem is to instal meters for all consumer categories.

On one item at least — street lighting — ZESCO is being paid for more power than it delivers. While district councils pay a fixed charge for estimated electricity consumed, in most cases street lights do not work because bulbs have either not been replaced or been broken by vandals.

Chapter 811, Part IV, Section 31 of the Laws of Zambia stipulates that it is an offence to consume electricity illegally. Hitherto, nobody has been prosecuted for theft of power. Any person who is guilty of an offence under the provisions of this Act shall be liable, in respect of each offence, (a) to a fine not exceeding one thousand Kwacha; (b) to imprisonment for a period not exceeding two years; (c) in default of payment of any fine imposed under the provisions, to imprisonment for a period not exceeding two years; or (d) to both such imprisonment and any such fine.

Conclusions and recommendations

The losses in the turbines should now be lower than those found during data collection. This is because of a rehabilitation of the Kafue Gorge turbines last year. The government should allocate foreign exchange to ZESCO to enable it to carry out rehabilitation of turbines. The losses due to wear and tear of the turbines are high compared to rehabilitation costs.

The overall level of losses is low. During the financial year 1987/1988 losses in the retail system were 4 per cent and 12.9 per cent in the north and south respectively. High voltage losses were 3.9 per cent. The overall losses were 6.5 per cent. These losses are lower than the 10 per cent average for developed countries.

Retail losses comprise technical and non-technical losses. During the 1987/1988 financial year the energy losses in the distribution and supply system amounted to 202 gwh which converts to a financial loss of K14.14 million at an average tariff of 7 ngwee per kwh. This is a substantial figure, and it is necessary to establish ways of minimising these losses. It was not easy to quantify, within this figure, the magnitude of theft of power. Although theft of power is a criminal offence, ZESCO does not take legal action against offenders because the legal process is costly and cumbersome. Those who are found stealing power are disconnected and re-connection is only effected when payment is made for energy estimated to have been consumed but not metered. Policy makers should recommend amendments to the Electricity Act so that offenders are punished heavily to discourage theft.

Meter reading is a very critical area for the utility. Unless all the meters are read properly, substantial losses are bound to occur. ZESCO should introduce incentive schemes for meter readers to increase productivity in this area.

There is no doubt that losses can be reduced if the measures recommended above are implemented. A reduction in losses would have no impact on tariffs, as such adjustments are considered an after event of the financial year. Only the cash flow would be affected — and positively. Meanwhile, further research work needs to be done in the important area of theft.

4.5 Hydro-electricity and Peat as Alternatives to Fuel Oil in the Industrial Sector in Burundi

Isaie Ntirizoshira

Burundi is a small country in Central Africa, lying between 2° 18′ and 4° 28′ of southern latitude and between 28° 50′ and 30° 53′ of eastern longitude. It faces a very critical economic situation proceeding from many factors:

- Its geographical location: Burundi is an enclaved country. Thus the transportation costs and various taxes raised by countries crossed by imported products make the latter very expensive. This is the case for petroleum products which play an important role in a country's economy, as energy inputs for industries and fuel for the transportation sector. Locally manufactured goods are then costly to produce (in part as a consequence of the expensive energy input) and are not competitive.
- Its overpopulation, combined with the fact that about 95 per cent of the population live in rural areas in a very traditional economic system. Farmers produce goods mainly to meet their nourishment needs and sell the eventual surplus. That is the main reason why Burundi's economy is not very efficient.
- Lack of natural resources: except for very small deposits of gold (manually extracted), Burundi has almost no natural resources. Nickel has been discovered recently, but its exploitation is not feasible under existing international market conditions. So foreign exchange accrues mainly from the export of agricultural products (coffee, tea, etc.).

Consequently, the improvement of Burundi's economy necessitates co-ordinated action in all sectors to induce dynamic economic activity. Steps to be taken include increased education and compulsory schooling up to a certain age (in order to ensure a minimum literacy level), encouragement of rurally based industries (processing agricultural products, for example), revival of the agricultural sector (by introducing high-yield seeds, providing guidance to farmers, etc.) and import substitution policies wherever possible. Some of these actions (schooling programmes, high-yield seed introduction, training of agricultural technicians, etc.) are in course of implementation and must be sustained, while others are still under study.

Because very little foreign exchange is earned by exports, import of goods results in a significant balance of payments deficit which can be reduced by substituting imported goods by locally available ones. Petroleum products imports, for example, account for about 20 per cent of all imports and drain nearly 30 per cent of foreign exchange accruing from exports. Some projects under study (ethanol production in sugar mills, methane utilisation) aim to reduce the share of petroleum products in the transportation sector and may have practical results. This paper analyses the technical possibility and financial feasibility of substituting imported fuel oil by domestic energy sources (electricity and peat) in the industrial sector.

Electricity and peat can be used in place of fuel oil in some industrial processes such as steam or hot water generation. A comparison of technologies using fuel oil, electricity and peat will demonstrate the technical possibility of the substitution. Then a financial analysis will compare present cost values, and provide levels of fuel prices at which electricity and peat systems can compete with fuel oil sets. The comparison of the computed and actual prices will show whether or not electricity and peat can compete with fuel oil under an actual pricing system, and lead to conclusions and suggestions for policy measures necessary to encourage a possible substitution.

Energy availability and supply reliability

According to a recent survey, industries operated by fuel oil need an input power of 10 mw. Thus, beside the actual market, electricity and peat supply should be able to meet an additional 10 mw demand.

Electricity

The economically exploitable hydro-power potential has been estimated at about 300 mw while the actual installed capacity amounts to 30 mw. Furthermore, most of the important industries are located in Bujumbura (the capital of the country), which had a 17 mw peak-power demand in 1987. Even though economic activity has increased rapidly during these last years in Gitega (the second city), Bujumbura is expected to be the main economic centre for a long time. That is the reason why the supply reliability study will focus on Bujumbura, which gets its electricity from three hydro-power plants: Mugere (8 mw) through a 35 kv transmission line; Rwegura (18 mw) through a 110 kv transmission line; and Ruzizi I (property of Zaire), which can deliver 10 mw at a low rate (about 4FBu/kwh) according to a long-term agreement between Burundi and Zaire. In the near future, two additional power plants are expected to come on line. Ruzizi II (40 mw in 1989) is the common property of three states (Zaire, Burundi and Rwanda) which will each get a third of the energy produced. Kagunuzi C (246 mw in 1995) will also provide water for irrigation purposes. Other power plants (Kagunuzi A and B, Masango, Rushiha) are also projected and may come on line whenever needed.

Gitega gets its electrical energy from a 1.275 mw hydro-power plant. By 1990, when it will be connected by a 110 kv transmission line to the high voltage grid supplying Bujumbura, it will no longer experience electricity shortages. All in all, Burundi can rely on an assured electricity supply, even if all industries shift from fuel oil to electrical energy.

Peat

The country's proven peat reserves amount to 40 million tons, with 30 per cent moisture and a heating value of about 3,000 kcal/kg. Besides, there is a sizeable peat bog on the border with Rwanda which has not been fully explored and may contain about 150 million tons of peat.

If all the industries operated by fuel oil were to shift to peat (with a utilisation factor of 0.7), they would require 61.32 gwh per year, that is about 220,750 gigajoules. The supply of this energy would entail the combustion of about 27,000 tons of peat per year (assuming 65 per cent efficiency for a peat-fired boiler). If urban households adopt peat for their cooking energy needs, an additional demand of about 40,000 tons can be expected. Since existing demand is 15,000 tons per year, total annual demand would then be 82,000 tons of peat: the proven reserves can sustain such demand for a very long time.

Technology comparison

Reliable technology is available for producing steam or hot water by means of fuel oil, natural gas, coal, lignite, peat or electricity. Solid, liquid and gas fuel-fired boilers are classified into three categories: watertube, firetube and cast iron boilers, all of which can be designed to burn any of the above fuels. The main difference between boilers lies in the combustion techniques:

- burners for gas and liquid fuels and pulverised solid fuels (average diameter for liquid and pulverised particles = 0.05 mm);
- stokers for roughly ground solid fuels (average particle diameter = 6 mm);
- fluidised beds with 1.5 mm average particle size.

Furthermore, given the lower heating value of solid fuels (heating value = 10,000 kcal/kg for oil, 6,500 kcal/kg for coal, and 3,000 kcal/kg for peat), solid fuel-fired furnaces are much larger than oil-burning furnaces delivering the same energy output. Besides, combustion of solid fuels requires additional systems such as fuel handling, grinding and storage facilities, bottom ash and fly ash handling equipment, and sulphur dioxide suppression systems to avoid pollution.

Heat generation by means of electric furnaces is also a well-tried technology, and four basic methods are used:

- resistance heating, where voltage is directly applied to a resister which provides heat by joule effect;
- induction heating, where electrically conductive materials (such as metal pieces) are immersed in an alternating magnetic field generated by an helectrical coil energised by a suitable a.c. energy source (operating frequencies range from 60 to 1,000 hz);
- dielectric heating, where high-frequency voltage (1 to 200 mhz) is applied to a non-conducting material; and

- microwave heating, which is based on the same principle as dielectric heating, but operates at higher frequencies (915 mhz and 2,450 mhz).

The first method is the easiest and the cheapest, and the only one to be considered for steam or hot water generation.

Cost evaluation

The cost comparison is based on a 1 mw boiler with a utilisation factor of 0.70. This entails the consumption of 6,132,000 kwh (22,075 gigajoules). Considered efficiencies are: 0.8 for a fuel oil boiler, 0.95 for an electric boiler and 0.65 for a peat boiler.

For each of the three technologies, the total cost can be broken down into 3 main components:

$I(i)$ = investment cost for technology i.
(When discounting, investment expenditures are assumed to occur in year 0.)
$O(i)$ = annual operation and maintenance cost for technology i.
$F(i)$ = annual fuel costs for technology i.

i = 1 for fuel oil technology.
i = 2 for electricity technology.
i = 3 for peat technology.

If $O1(i)$ is the sum of discounted operation and maintenance costs and $F1(i)$ the sum of the discounted fuel costs during the lifetime of technology, the present value of the total cost can be expressed as follows:

$$C(i) = I(i) + O1(i) + F1(i)$$

where $F1(2)$ and $F1(3)$ are the only unknowns. By equating $C(1)$ to $C(2)$, and $C(1)$ to $C(3)$ we obtain values for $F(i)$ and $F(3)$ (that is the present values of total fuel cost for electricity and peat), from which we can compute electricity and peat prices allowing competitiveness of these two fuels with fuel oil.

Comparative costs
1. Fuel oil boiler:
   - investment costs (including purchasing, freight and installation costs): US$80,000
   - Operation and maintenance (5 per cent of investment costs): US$4,000
   - Fuel costs: a 1 mw fuel oil boiler with a utilisation of 0.7 and an efficiency of 0.8 will burn about 689,850 kg of fuel. Since fuel oil costs US$0.46/kg, the annual fuel costs are estimated at US$317,331. Assuming a 20-year lifetime for the equipment and a 10 per cent discount rate, the present value of the total cost for the fuel oil technology is US$2,826,508.

2. Peat-fired boiler:
   - Investment costs (purchasing of the boiler and all necessary equipment needed to deal with solid fuel combustion, their freight and installation costs): US$300,000.
   - Operation and maintenance costs (5 per cent of investment costs): US$15,000. Assuming the same conditions as for the fuel oil boiler (20-year lifetime and 10 per cent discount rate), the present value of the known costs is US$401,276.
3. Electric boiler:
   - Investment costs = US$60,000.
   - Operation and maintenance costs = US$3,000.
   - The present value of the known costs is US$80,255.

So the present value of the fuel costs allowing competitiveness of peat and electricity are:

$F1(2) = 2,826,508 - 80,255 = 2,746,253$ (US$) for electricity and,
$F1(3) = 2,826,508 - 401,276 = 2,425,232$ (US$) for peat.

This translates into an annual fuel cost of US$283,743 for peat, or US$321,301 for electricity. On the other hand, assuming 0.65 efficiency for a peat boiler and 0.95 for an electric boiler, the annual energy requirements are about 6,454,740 kwh of electrical energy or 33,961,540,000 kilojoules proceeding from the combustion of 2,705,000 kg of peat. Thus the fuel costs at which the three technologies have the same discounted total cost (that is, the maximum cost allowing competitiveness of fuel oil, peat and electricity) are US$0.05 (equivalent to 7.5FBu) per kwh for electricity and US$0.10 (equivalent to 15FBu) per kwh for peat (1 US$ = 150FBu).

The above investment, operation and maintenance costs are approximate values and may be slightly different from the actual ones. But the main results (that is, electricity and peat prices allowing competitiveness with fuel oil) still hold, because investment costs account for a very small share (less than 5 per cent) of the present value of total costs.

Electricity and peat pricing

Peat is actually sold at 8FBu per kg. A World Bank study has determined a cost of 4.89FBu per kg if annual production is increased to 28,000 tons and 4.29FBu/kg for a 59,000 ton annual production (the actual production is about 15,000 tons per year).

For low voltage consumers, the present electricity price is 13.5FBu/kwh. For medium voltage consumers, the electricity price comprises two components:

- a fixed premium of 6,000FBu/year per kilowatt of subscribed power;
- a proportional component of 12FBu/kwh for 150 hours monthly utilisation (assumed to correspond to peak period consumption), and 8.5FBu/kwh for the rest of the utilisation period (assumed to correspond to off-peak period).

86 Electricity

The electricity utility is considering the introduction of appropriate meters (giving consumptions during peak and off-peak period) in order to charge 12FBu/kwh for peak-period consumption and 8.5FBu/kwh for off-peak consumption.

Conclusions

Under actual electricity pricing, electricity does not constitute a feasible substitute for fuel oil in water and steam generation. This is due to the fact that hydro-power is exploited through a highly capital-intensive technology.

On the other hand, peat offers real opportunities of reducing fuel oil use in the industrial sector. Its availability and low cost make it very attractive for industrial managers and may allow a short payback period. In the case, for example, of COTEBU textile plant (owned by the government) which uses 2 mw fuel oil boilers, a switch to peat technology could lead to substantial savings. Procurement and installation of two 1 mw boilers and associated systems are estimated at about US$600,000 (90 million FBu). Assuming the same operation conditions as estimated above (0.7 utilisation factor, 0.8 efficiency for fuel oil boiler and 0.65 efficiency for peat boiler), the annual fuel costs would be 43.28 million FBu for peat when they amount to 76.15 million FBu for fuel oil. So the shift from fuel oil to peat would result in 32.87 million FBu annual savings in fuel costs, and the payback period would be less than 3 years. Steps should be taken in order to substitute fuel oil by peat in those industries that make most use of fuel oil. In fact, the government should introduce peat-fired technology in COTEBU textile plant and demonstrate to entrepreneurs that substitution of fuel oil by peat is very profitable. Initial cost (procurement and installation of peat-fired boilers) may be high for small and medium-sized industries, so the government should analyse possibilities of facilitating acquisition of the equipment (by reducing taxes, for example).

5 Coal and Gasification

5.1 Options for Power Generation in Somalia

Isse Ali Ahmed

This study is a comparative analysis of various power supply options available to Somalia through three sources: imported oil, coal, and imported electricity. The study will contribute to research on energy and will help policy-makers to decide on the relative merits of the different power generation options. The data base on energy supply and demand is poor: much time was spent collecting data for systematic analysis in the study.

Background to the problem area

Somalia depends heavily on electricity generation using diesel engines. Most of the regional and district towns are supplied with electric power by diesel generators ranging in size from 60 to 1500 kva. There is only one small hydro-electric power source in the south, generating limited power to one district town.

In Mogadishu there are two diesel stations that burn heavy fuel oil and one steam unit fired in the same way. In all towns except Mogadishu electricity is supplied for part of the day only. Breakdowns are frequent and spare parts to repair and maintain the small-scale power units are often unavailable.

Electricity tariffs are far from adequate: though diesel fuel prices have increased by 500 per cent over the last three years, these increases have not been passed on to the consumer. As a result ENEE (National Electricity Utility) has operated at a loss in recent years.

Clearly, Somalia needs to consider the options available to provide cheap and reliable power to the consumers. This study addresses some issues and options that apply particularly to towns in the north of the country. The research objectives are:

1. To collect existing information on power generation in specific locations.
2. To estimate the demand forecast using demographic and economic variables.
3. On this demand forecast, to project the necessary power supply.
4. To calculate the capital cost of the machines required to meet the demand in each of three proposed systems.
5. Finally, to compare the tariffs that would result from the three systems.

One of the options available in the north is imported electricity and the only possible supplier is Ethiopia. Ethiopia can supply the northern regions because transmission lines already extend as far as Djibouti and can be extended into Somalia.

Present electricity supply

Demand and supply levels in Somalia are very low: total energy consumption is estimated at 26 kwh per capita per annum. Almost all the electricity is generated by thermal plants. The exception is the 4.8 mw hydro-power plant commissioned in 1983 at Jelib on the Juba river.

The supply of electricity in Mogadishu and seven regional centres is administered by ENEE. In all the other regions supply is controlled by the various municipalities. The capacity of the power generators in Mogadishu is about 57 mw. Stations in Kismayo and Baidoa, both commissioned in 1987, deliver 2 mw and 1.7 mw respectively. At Bossaso, Erigavo and Qardo power stations are under construction.

The four northern regions are among those whose electricity supply is controlled by ENEE. Power in these regions comes from small diesel generators using expensive light fuel diesel oil. The northern regions, like all others, have electricity for only part of the day due to the shortage of fuel.

Electricity systems in four northern regional centres

1. Berbera
Berbera, the second largest port in the country, exports livestock and has an international airport. A cement plant is also located there which produces 600 tons of cement per day. The population of Berbera is about 165,000 and it is a growing commercial centre. The available power supply in this district is 2,393 kw and the forecast maximum demand by 1990, including the cement plant, is 11,000 kw. Other small plants — like one producing gypsum — generate their own power.

2. Borama
Borama, situated 140 km west of Hargeisa, is largely an agricultural area. The population is 60,000. The present available power capacity is 225 kw and the maximum demand forecast for the year 1990 is 1,694 kw.

3. Buroa
Buroa is situated 140 km from Berbera. The area is largely dependent on livestock and has a population of 80,000. The available power is 1,800 kw and the maximum demand forecast for the year 1990 is 3,007 kw.

4. Hargeisa
Hargeisa is Somalia's second largest city and is situated nearly 170 km from Berbera. The available power capacity is 3,790 kw and the maximum demand for the year 1990 is 6,569 kw.

Load forecast

Table 1 below forecasts 1990 electricity demand in northern regional centres, assuming that the following factors remain constant:

1. Population (initial population, population growth and immigration rate).
2. Domestic consumption. The number of consumers is calculated as the number of households that would be supplied at the present connection rate. The number of households is calculated as the total population divided by the number of people in an average household (7 people). The consumption of low-income households is assumed to be 450 kwh, that of high-income households to be 800 kwh.
3. Consumption by commercial firms, light industries and government offices.
4. Consumption for military purposes, water pumping and street lighting.
5. Losses.

Table 1
1990 electricity demand in northern regional centres
(in kw)

Towns	Hargeisa	Borama	Buroa	Berbera	Total
Demand	6,569	1,694	3,007	11,016	22,286
Installed	3,790	225	1,800	2,393	8,208
Request	2,779	1,469	1,800	1,207	14,078

Source: Kennedy and Donkin, *Somalia Power Planning Study*.

Development options

In the northern regional centres demand will be 23 mw of power in 1990 while the installed capacity in that year will be only 8 mw. An additional power supply of 20 mw will be needed to meet the growing needs of these towns. The power should either be imported from Ethiopia or generated by new thermal plants with added capacities.

Main findings: comparative costs

The capital, fuel and other costs of steam and gas turbines using diesel as a fuel, a diesel generator using H.F. oil as a fuel, and a steam turbine using coal as a fuel have been compared in Table 2 overleaf.

Due to the high cost of the imported oil, gas and steam turbines have become more expensive than steam power using imported coal and diesel engines using H.F. oil as a fuel. Coal is more economic in all the power generation schemes.

Electricity tariffs in previous years show that they are greatly influenced

Table 2
Comparative costs of four power generation systems

System	Capital cost (US$m)	Life (years)	Variable O & M cost $/mwhso		Fixed O & M cost		US $/ 1 kwh
			Fuel	O*M	Staff	Other	
Steam (oil fired) (15 mw)	15.75	25	52.00	1.10	0.24	0.16	0.062
Gas turbine (15 mw)	5.88	15	69.91	4.10	0.89	0.05	0.081
Steam (coal fired) (25 mw)	20.3		Annual capital cost 2.03		Annual opr. cost 2.67 (est.)		0.028
Diesel (H.F. oil) (2 x 15 mw)	32.0		Annual capital cost 3.84		Annual opr. cost 5.06		0.048

Sources: Kennedy and Donkin, *Power Planning Study* (steam and gas turbines); Chinese manufacturer (coal-fired steam turbine); BWSC, *Diesel Power Plant*, 1988.

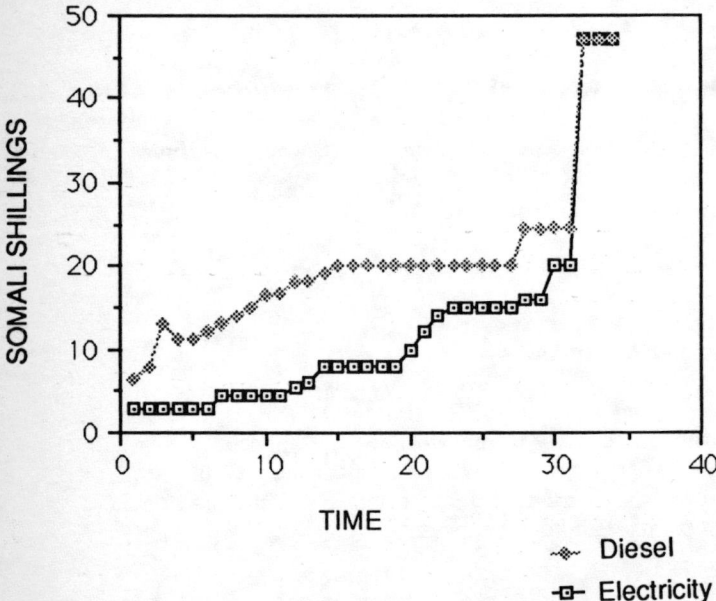

Figure 1. Changes of electricity tariffs and diesel price

by changes in fuel prices and exchange rates. Figure 1 shows that electricity tariffs do not change immediately due to delay in government decisions to increase tariffs in relation to prevailing prices of imported fuel. But at the end of 1988, electricity tariffs increased by 208 per cent as diesel fuel prices went up by 130 per cent: to understand this hike it is necessary to consider the long-run marginal cost of electricity supply in the country.

Table 3
Prices of imported petroleum products and coal

	Kennedy & Donkin estimate	Actual price 1988
Diesel	200 US$/ton	198 US$/ton
H.F. oil	150 US$/ton	173 US$/ton
Coal	50 US$/ton	—

Sources: Kennedy and Donkin, *Somalia Power Planning Study*; petroleum co-operatives (actual prices).

Its comparatively low cost as a resource for power generation and the existence of small deposits in the northern regions make coal an attractive source for power generation in Somalia. A study made by the Federal Republic of Germany showed sufficient coal (2.5 million tons) of suitable quality (net calorific value greater than 3,500 kcal/gram) to supply a 20 mw power station for a period of at least 15 years. The deposits are yet to be tested, except for one located close to the northern towns.

Now that political relations with Ethiopia have improved, Somalia is to consider the possibility of importing electricity from its neighbour. It is proposed to examine the cost of importing electricity through Djibouti. However, there are two main constraints: installation and maintenance of the transmission lines through hilly terrain will be costly, and the transmission losses will be as high as 20 per cent due to the distances involved. Under these circumstances the study concludes that the government should (a) improve maintenance of existing thermal stations; and (b) develop new coal-based power stations in the north.

References

Edwin and Partners, *Electric Power in the Northern Regions* (1980).
Kennedy and Donkin, *Power Planning Study* (1986).
Ministry of Planning, *Performance in the Somali Economy* (1983–87).
Pakistan Ltd, *Electric Power Supply in the Southern Regions* (1980).

5.2 Issues and Prospects for Coal Utilisation in Zimbabwe's Rural Households

Ruzvidzo S. Maya
(in collaboration with Naomi N. Wekwete)

The increasing shortage of traditional fuels in Zimbabwe has prompted government to consider seriously the use of coal in rural households. In this regard, both government and the privately owned coal industry have begun pilot projects in selected rural areas to initiate the introduction of coal stoves and coal fuels.

To date, over six hundred stoves have been distributed to rural households. About 135 of these were supplied free as part of a government-led pilot project. The rest were sold by Lakas Products Pvt. Ltd, a coal merchant, and by the Wankie Colliery Company, a coal producer.

These efforts by government and the coal industry need to be informed by knowledge of the financial and economic dimensions of coal diffusion to rural economies, the environmental implications of widespread coal use in rural households, and the general acceptability of coal as a fuel to households with a long tradition of free fuels.

This report summarises the results of a study undertaken to provide such background information. Conducted over six months during 1988, the study included field surveys of four districts in Zimbabwe: Murewa, Shurugwi, Mberengwa, and Mazoe Citrus Estates. All but the Mazoe district are rural settings with severe shortages of fuelwood. Mazoe Citrus Estates is a semi-urban plantation community which has had over twenty years' experience with coal use in households under a company-sponsored programme which supplies both fuels and stoves free of charge.

During surveys in these districts the study sought to gain insight into the imperatives of coal diffusion by considering the following factors: cost, environmental hazard, smoke emissions, constraining attitudes, marketing options.

To study environmental factors, notably household exposure to toxic emissions, the study assessed coal handling practices in rural household settings, stove designs, and ventilation features in typical houses, among other factors. To assess acceptability, the study analysed a number of factors including the coal pricing system, the income base of the rural household, alternative coal delivery systems, and the cost of coal stoves.

All these assessments were made against the background of the present level of coal utilisation in rural households, present experience with commercial fuels, and levels of wood shortage in the districts studied. The shortage of wood for fuel was measured by distance travelled to fetch wood as an indication of the severity of the shortage. Coal utilisation in rural households is at present very limited. In 1987, 72,000 tonnes of coal were used in households throughout the country. Of this quantity 40,000 tonnes were bought by institutions such as schools and hospitals for use in employee households. The remaining 32,000 were used by other households including rural ones. The exact quantity used by the latter could not be assessed because we were unable to run a complete census of users, and sales figures from merchants did not provide complete information in this regard. The sketchy information available indicates a very low level of utilisation. In 1987, the Wankie Colliery Company supplied 10 tonnes to a depot in Murewa. The same company supplies 90 kg of coal per month to each household on its Mazoe Citrus plantation.

Of the 799 households surveyed, 266 (28 per cent) owned coal stoves, 81 had used coal for more than five years, and 116 had owned coal stoves for periods ranging from 2 to 5 years. The other respondents had had stoves for less than two years. A number of these had received their stoves from government or other institutions as part of a pilot or other sponsored project. One must note here that the majority of those with coal stoves are on the Mazoe Citrus Estates. If we exclude this district from the analysis, it will be apparent that coal and coal stove use in rural Zimbabwe is very limited. Only 36 rural households own stoves. Of these 36, 22 paid for their stoves.

Direct purchase of coal stoves in the rural households has not been a major form of diffusion for the technology. There were some households in the survey who had prior experience with coal use in non-rural settings. They were willing to obtain stoves but, like nearly everyone else, did not get around to doing so. In general, people responded negatively for many and various reasons. We identified three major ones, however: lack of knowledge regarding the coal alternative, i.e. lack of initiative on the part of the households and the authorities to confront the coal option; lack of access to coal stoves or unavailability of these; and the cost of stoves and of the coal fuel.

These conclusions are based on responses to open questions giving reasons for not using coal and coal stoves. The survey also sought to assess factors which have been considered influential in the decision whether or not to adopt the coal option. These are perception of hazard, traditional or social inertia, the shortage of wood as the traditional fuel, cost, and environmental factors.

Perception of hazard

It is generally argued, following a number of coal-related toxifications, that rural households are averse to the use of coal, and would reject it as a domestic fuel, because of the hazard factor. The survey sought first to establish the existence of this perception of hazard, and then to establish the degree to which it affected household decisions on the use of coal.

Our findings were that 62 per cent of the surveyed households were ignorant of the health hazards associated with coal utilisation. Only 4 per cent of the respondents would treat coal hazards as a serious factor in deciding whether or not to adopt it for household use. The rest of the respondents were aware of the hazards of coal but would not reject its use for this reason. Even the 4 per cent who would consider hazard as a factor would not categorically rule out coal for this reason.

Statistical analysis also showed very poor correlations between the perception of hazard and the predisposition of rural households to accept or reject coal. Thus the perception of hazard, hitherto considered a major impediment to the diffusion of coal as a rural household fuel, did not turn out, on these results, to have any significant bearing on the acceptance or rejection of coal.

Tradition

Western and even local literature is replete with *prima facie* statements claiming that rural people in Africa are averse to change due to their strong adherence to traditional ways and beliefs. The study did not find that any traditional or social considerations affected the acceptability of coal.

Questions asked in this regard included those on traditional attributes, on the comparative cleanliness and tendency to smoke of coal and wood, on comparative ignition difficulties and on heating properties under rural cooking conditions. Answers to these questions were of limited significance for the majority of rural households who had had no prior experience with coal. Only respondents from the Mazoe Citrus area and the few other rural residents with prior coal experience could offer a meaningful judgment on the question.

Of the 404 who had previous experience, 293 (or 73 per cent) generally preferred coal to wood. Sixty believed coal cooked faster than wood, 49 expressly noted that coal stoves were more efficient as cooking devices than open wood fires, 38 preferred coal specifically because wood was getting scarce, and another 38 preferred coal because it emitted less smoke once ignited.

On the other hand, 111 respondents, 27 per cent of those who had prior experience with coal, preferred wood. Eleven of these attributed their preference to the initial ignition difficulty of coal, 31 others cited the toxic effects of coal, and another 31 cited cost.

The shortage of wood

Our initial feeling was that the increasing shortage of wood would predispose people to accept coal as an alternative fuel. In the study, it was apparent that there was an increasing severity of wood shortage in Murewa, Mberengwa, and Shurugwi. The reforestation programme offered absolutely no alternative at the time of study. People thus had begun to use purchased wood, roots and dung, as well as traversing borders to resettlement areas to collect wood over long distances. The results of our analysis indicate very little correlation between distance travelled, a proxy for wood shortage, and preference for coal. This was a puzzle which we could not explain. It seemed to indicate either an element of irrationality in the behaviour of rural households, or the inadequacy of our proxy for wood shortage.

The element of cost

Cost was analysed in terms of affordability, i.e. the ability of households to pay for coal stoves, and in terms of price for coal and stoves.

To assess ability to pay we considered the income base of the rural households. A few factors were apparent. The area studied had an average per capita income of $75 (1987). This income exhibited an uneven distribution over the year, peaking in July and August after grain sales, and troughing in December and January after planting and school expenses. It also happened that the period of peak income coincided with the period of access to crop residues utilisable for fuel, and that the troughing period coincided with the period when crop residues have vanished due to ploughing down and use as fuel.

Second, the rural households have no access to credit facilities for buying hardware, particularly hardware without a direct bearing on production. For this reason they would have to pay cash for stoves which range in price from $74.23 to $463.20. This is a very inhibitive factor. The cost of fuel coal per year for a six-member family, by our estimates, would be $121.20 per year for Murewa. This would come down by as much as 40 per cent if bulk delivery of coal was instituted and the present 12.5 per cent tax removed completely.

Either way, the cost of fuel would not be easily borne by the rural household, at least not throughout the year. The pricing of coal is based on a build-up typified by a high transport component, sales tax, and rather high dealer mark-ups. There can be very little improvement on the current build-up besides tax concessions and bulk deliveries with decanting done at the sales depot.

Environmental factors

As stated earlier, the known hazards of coal utilisation did not deter households from positive consideration of the coal alternative. Environmental danger could be exacerbated by certain practices of households and by some attributes of fuel coal. In assessing the possibility of this danger we paid particular attention to carbon dioxide poisoning and sulphur dioxide exposure.

Practices with a bearing on such events include ventilation, draft control on stoves, use of kitchens as bedrooms and the quality of coal used.

Out of the 799 households surveyed (total estimated population of 5,593), 36 per cent reported sleeping in the kitchen at night. Of these, 77 per cent slept in poorly ventilated kitchens. Sixteen per cent had kitchens attached to bedrooms, and 50 per cent adhered to the practice of not extinguishing the fire after use at night.

These figures enable us to estimate that about 28 per cent of people represented by the surveyed households are at risk in terms of carbon dioxide toxification. Of these some would be in a high-risk category — those who used coal for warmth generation during cold months. This category may include those who do not currently use kitchens for bedrooms but may do so during cold months.

Sulphur dioxide exposure would be generalised to all households, either inside the kitchen if plume dispersal fittings on the stove are poor or in the outside environment as plume dispersal would occur just above ground level because of low flue pipes. Ash disposal would also be a problem in the probable absence of a central properly built ash disposal pit.

Conclusion

There are no serious attitudinal impediments to the diffusion of the coal stove technology in rural households. There are, however, serious financial limitations unless government combines coal diffusion with programmes to strengthen the rural income base. Environmental consequences could be severe unless proper building standards are enforced and stove designs ensure safe dispersal of flue gases.

5.3 Coal Resources Availability in Botswana: An Assessment of Present and Future Demand

M. P. Modisi

Southern Africa, and Botswana in particular, is well-endowed with relatively large reserves of coal. The existence of coal in Botswana has been known since the end of the last century. Exploration activities by the Geological Survey and the private sector led to the discovery of major deposits and by the late 1960s reserves capable of supporting a mine at Morupule for the domestic market had been confirmed. The oil crises of 1973—74 and 1978—79 stimulated increased interest in coal exploration the world over and Botswana attracted several private sector companies looking for coal that could be traded on the international market. As a result vast resources and reserves of low to medium quality bituminous coal, suitable for the export market, were proved. Resources amounting to 21,680 million tonnes of *in situ* coal had been revealed by 1987. Reserves of possible economic exploitation are estimated at 10,180 million tonnes in two coal field areas, namely the Morupule Coal Field and the Mmamabula Coal Field. Since the collapse of oil prices and consequently coal prices in the mid-1980s, enthusiasm for coal exploration has plummeted and relatively little prospecting has taken place.

The coal occurs within the Upper Carboniferous to Jurassic Karoo Supergroup which underlies some 60 per cent of the country's land surface. The western part of the country is mantled by the 'Kalahari' beds, a top layer of unconsolidated sands masking bedrock geology. Although coal seams have been intersected in boreholes in this western area, most exploration activity has taken place in the eastern part of the country where the Morupule and Mmamabula coal fields are located. It is in the east that most of the population is concentrated and infrastructure has been developed.

It is against this background of existing proven coal deposits that this study has been carried out. What is necessary now is to inspect the demand for coal in order to help policy makers to plan for the utilisation of this energy resource. An introductory resource evaluation from the demand side is therefore provided in the study. The deposits are classed according to the degree of geological assurance. It has become apparent that consideration must be given to the utilisation of coal in the domestic market, as well as for electric power generation and the smelting of copper/nickel ore. To this end, the demand for coal in households and institutions is examined. The prospect of making coal accessible to these latter sectors introduces a further policy option — to open a mine closer to demand centres in the populated areas of south-east Botswana. Finally, some of the environmentally undesirable qualities of coal, e.g. exposure to sulphur dioxide, may be reduced by establishing a coal beneficiating plant.

Resources and reserves

The original exploration reports prepared by the private sector show that different procedures for calculating coal reserves were used. Variations include the different criteria used for the definition of seam margins, borehole sampling interval, inclusion and exclusion of dirt partings and the interpretation of what is the economic width of the coal seam. Figures for *in situ* coal reserves and quality are taken as they are from exploration reports. In order to bring some level of uniformity to these data, a classification of the deposits was carried out according to degrees of geological assurance in resource and reserve estimates.

Table 1 shows the criteria used to classify deposits. Proven reserves are those for which further exploration is not required for mine planning. Feasibility and pre-feasibility studies have been undertaken, however, on deposits which fall under probable, indicated and inferred reserves. Table 2 is a summary of coal resources and reserves according to criteria shown in Table 1. The deposits are located in two main areas, namely, the Morupule Coal Area with resources amounting to 10,660 million tonnes and economic reserves of 4,360 million tonnes, and the Mmamabula Coal Area with resources amounting to 11,020 million tonnes and reserves of 5,820 million tonnes.

The quality of run-of-mine (ROM) coal from Morupule Colliery is shown in Table 3. The figures are obtained from samples taken on different days to provide an indication of the variability. The Botswana Power Corporation requires a supply that has a calorific value of not less than 22.1 mj/kg and sulphur of not more than 2.5 per cent. The size range should be less than 31.5 mm, but 35 per cent must not be less than 3.2 mm. The coal at Morupule easily meets these requirements.

Production

Morupule Colliery, the only coal mine in Botswana, has been producing a steadily increasing annual tonnage which was 294,039 tonnes in 1977 and 579,409 tonnes in 1987, virtually doubling over a ten-year period. The bulk of the production is consumed in electric power generation.

Demand

Three main demand sectors for coal can be defined on the domestic market, namely (1) generation of electric power; (2) government institutions and households; and (3) industrial plants. Export potential will be disregarded at this stage because of the low level of coal prices on the international market and lack of suitable infrastructure.

Table 1
Classification criteria according to borehole density and spacing

Class of resource	No. of boreholes per km^2	Borehole spacing in km
Proven	More than 10	Less than 0.3
Probable	10–1	0.3–1
Indicated	1–0.4	1–3
Inferred	0.4–0.2	3–5
Hypothetical	0.2–0.04	5–10
Speculative	Less than 0.04	More than 10

Table 2
Summary of Botswana coal resources and reserves
(million tonnes)

Coal field Deposit	Reserves Measured					Resources			Total
	Proven	Probable	Indicated	Inferred	Subtotal	Hypothetical	Speculative	Subtotal	
Morupule coal area									
Morupule mine lease	40	55	—	—	95	3,200	—	3,200	3,295
Lease 12/82A	—	—	1,080	5	1,085	—	—	—	1,085
Kagswe	—	1,890	390	—	2,280	100	—	100	2,380
Lease 11/82	—	—	10	890	900	—	3,000	3,000	3,900
Subtotal	40	1,945	1,480	895	4,360	3,300	3,000	6,300	10,660
Mmamabula Coal Area									
Mmamabula Central	—	440	—	—	440	—	—	—	440
Mmamabula East	—	—	—	2,150	2,150	—	—	—	2,150
Mmamabula South	—	—	—	—	—	2,500	—	2,500	2,500
Areas of Cdf	—	—	—	3,230	3,230	—	—	—	3,230
Mmamabula/ Mmamantswe	—	—	—	—	—	600	—	600	600
Kweneng	—	—	—	—	—	—	2,100	2,100	2,100
Subtotal	—	440	—	5,380	5,820	3,100	2,100	5,200	11,020
Total	40	2,385	1,480	6,275	10,180	6,400	5,100	11,500	21,680

Source: Adapted from Botswana Energy Master Plan, 1987.

Table 3
ROM coal quality at Morupule Colliery

Date	Inherent moisture %	Ash %	Volatile matter %	Calorific value mj/kg	Sulphur %
15.11.84	3.7	24.8	17.0	24.70	1.87
15.02.85	5.1	22.8	18.2	23.97	1.61
19.10.85	3.6	23.5	17.5	24.76	1.50
15.03.86	4.7	23.2	18.2	23.94	0.87

Source: Ministry of Mineral Resources and Water Affairs (1987).

Electric power generation

In 1988, coal consumption for electric power generation was forecast as 450,000 tonnes. The demand up to 1994 is shown in Table 4. At Morupule Power Station, the consumption is at 0.6 tonnes coal per mwh and 0.78 tonnes coal per mwh at the Selebi Phikwe Power Station. The coal price charged to the Botswana Power Corporation at Morupule was Pula 19/tonne and Pula 29/tonne at Selebi Phikwe in 1988.

Government institutions and households

A coal utilisation study completed in 1986 concluded that the potential demand for coal in households and institutions would rise to some 80,000 tonnes in 1988 and double to some 161,000 tonnes by the year 2007. This demand was calculated using the relatively highly populated centres of eastern Botswana clustered around Francistown in the north and Gaborone in the south. Areas in the western part of the country were excluded mainly because of the poorly developed infrastructure for coal distribution and the relatively low population density. As a result of this study, the Botswana government established the Expanded Coal Utilisation Project (ECUP) which is charged with three main tasks aimed at stimulating the utilisation of coal in government institutions and households. The objective of the project is to substitute coal for the dwindling supply of fuelwood in the major population centres. This is a major undertaking: at present, fuelwood accounts for about 90 per cent of the country's household energy. The ECUP's tasks can be outlined as follows:

1. To carry out promotional activities alongside the introduction of coal in government institutions such as hospitals, health centres, schools and colleges.
2. To disseminate information which would make propaganda for the utilisation of coal in private households, primarily as a substitute for fuelwood.
3. To make strategic plans for the commercialisation and distribution of coal and for making it more accessible to small buyers.

The progress of the project will be reported to the Botswana government. It is, however, apparent from initial assessments that the project has verified the demand forecast in institutions and households.

Table 4
Demand forecast for Botswana Power Corporation

Year (ending March)	Tonnage	% increase
1989	453,000	
1990	505,000	11.5
1991	601,000	19.0
1992	637,000	6.0
1993	669,000	5.0
1994	704,000	5.0

Source: Information from Botswana Power Corporation, August 1988.

Table 5
Comparison of transportation costs for coal by railway wagon from Mmamabula and Morupule (based on haulage using 39-ton wagons by Botswana Railways, August 1988)

Destination	Transportation cost in Pula/ton from source		Cost in Pula/ton delivered at railhead ex-Morupule (adding Pula 21/ton coal at Morupule minehead)
	Mmamabula	Morupule	
Lobatse	7.15	15.86	36.86
Ramotswa	5.70	14.45	35.45
Gaborone	5.12	13.86	34.86
Pilane	4.14	12.71	33.71
Mahalapye	4.71	7.98	28.98
Palapye	6.84	1.92	22.92
Serule	9.15	7.98	28.98
Shashe	10.88	9.84	30.84
Francistown	11.46	10.56	31.56
Tshesebe	13.23	12.15	33.15

Industrial plants

The coal utilisation study has reported a consumption of about 29,200 tonnes of coal in industrial plants in 1985. By far the largest consumer is the Botswana Meat Commission which uses some 22,000 tonnes per annum. Other plants include the Kgalagadi Breweries and Botswana Breweries. A notable aspect in these plants is that the bulk of the coal consumed is imported because plant specifications require upgraded coal. Import of this coal amounts to 25,900 tonnes per annum. At present, Morupule coal is not upgraded. The establishment of a coal-upgrading plant would make import substitution possible. A supply of upgraded coal to government institutions and private households will provide a fuel with a higher heating value and reduced sulphur content. Such a product would be environmentally more acceptable.

In 1988, the Sua Pan soda ash project was expected to introduce a demand of about 150,000 tonnes of coal for the generation of electrical power. Morupule Colliery, which has ample capacity to meet increased demand, is expected to provide this coal.

Mmamabula option

The Mmamabula Central measured coal reserves amount to about 440 million tonnes, ideally located near the railway line some 170 km south of Morupule. Railway transportation costs, a major factor in pricing delivered coal, make the Mmamabula option an attractive proposition. This is true of demand centres located in the southern part of the country in and around Gaborone, Ramotswa and Lobatse. At these centres railway transportation costs would be reduced by half as demonstrated in Table 5. A coal mine at Mmamabula could also be an on-site supply for a power station which may be due for consideration in 1998.

Conclusion

Botswana possesses vast resources of coal amounting to some 21,680 million tonnes in the prospected areas of east-central Botswana. Reserves of possible economic exploitation are estimated at 10,180 million tonnes. As is customary in most developing countries, prospecting for mineral resources such as coal is conducted for purposes of export. Indeed, the coal resources of Botswana have been established partly with this purpose in mind. However, disillusionment with the capricious international coal market, lack of adequate rail transport infrastructure and the landlocked disposition of Botswana have put an end to export plans. Increased attention is focused on the utilisation of coal for domestic consumption. Morupule Colliery, the only producing mine in Botswana, has doubled its production between 1977 and 1987 to supply the domestic market. The bulk of this production is used for electric power generation and this trend will continue for the foreseeable future. Home-based electric power generation contributes towards the country's self-sufficiency in energy supply while improving the quality of life and industrial development.

The commissioning of the Morupule Power Station has drastically reduced dependency on imported electricity. Present policy dictates that imported electricity shall not exceed 25 per cent of peak demand. It is recommended that in future planning for electric power generation, consideration should be given to the Mmamabula Central coal deposits. This would provide a mine that is located closer to the population centres of southern Botswana and help reduce railway transportation costs for coal supplied to households, institutions and industrial plants.

Some 90 per cent of the energy needs in households is met by woodfuel. The free supply of this resource in and around the densely populated areas of eastern Botswana has run out. Commercialisation of fuelwood supply to urban areas and large villages has increased pressure to find an alternative energy fuel for households in densely populated areas. Coal could provide such an alternative. In order to increase the heating value and reduce some of the environmentally undesirable effects of coal burning, there is a need to establish a coal washing plant. Such a plant would also enable import substitution in such industrial plants as the Botswana Meat Commission and the breweries.

Bibliography

Boockcock, C. 1965. *Mineral Resources of the Bechuanaland Protectorate.* Bulletin No. 1, Geological Survey of Botswana, pp. 369—417.
Clark, G.C., Lock, N.P. and Smith, R.A. 1985. *Coal Resources of Botswana.* Special Publication No. 9, Geological Society, South Africa.
Department of Mines. 1985. Annual Report, 1984. Botswana Government.
Department of Mines. 1987. Annual Report, 1986. Botswana Government.
Ministry of Finance and Development Planning. 1985. National Development Plan,1985—91. Botswana Government.
Ministry of Mineral Resources and Water Affairs. 1985. Coal Utilisation Study, Part I, Market Research Summary (unpublished).
Ministry of Mineral Resources and Water Affairs. 1986. Coal Utilisation Study, Final Report, Vols I to III. Botswana Government (unpublished).
Ministry of Mineral Resources and Water Affairs. 1987. Botswana Energy Master Plan, Final Report, Vol. I. Botswana Government.
Silitshena, R.M.K. 1975. 'Coal mining in Botswana: resources exploitation for self-sufficiency'. *Zambia Geographical Journal,* Nos 29—30, pp.63—73.
Smith, R.A. 1984. *The Lithostratigraphy of the Karoo Supergroup in Botswana.* Bulletin No. 26, Geological Survey of Botswana.

5.4 The Influence of Comparative Price in the Substitution of Coal for Woodfuel and Charcoal: the Zambian Case

A.N. Ng'andu (in collaboration with A.M. Mwanza)

Existing energy supply and demand

Although Zambia is well endowed with energy resources — woodlands and forests, hydro-electricity and coal satisfy 88 per cent of the nation's needs — it still imports petroleum to meet the balance in the energy demand. Economic decline has had some major implications for the country's energy sector in that not only has it arrested the growth in energy demand, leaving many of the supply systems with excess capacity, but it has also starved the energy sector of foreign exchange for capital investment.

In the domestic energy scenario of Zambia in 1986, households were estimated to account for 58 per cent of final energy demand, the bulk of which is met primarily by wood (75 per cent) and charcoal (22 per cent). Population growth is rapid, averaging about 3.5 per cent annually, and urbanisation (and hence the use of charcoal) is increasing. Consequently wood consumption is rising rapidly, probably faster than population growth.

Estimates of the current sustainable yield of Zambia's woodlands (14 million cubic metres), and current consumption of woodfuels (14.4 million cubic metres) suggest that this demand is not causing rapid deforestation nationally (FAO, 1986). However, two aspects of Zambia's woodfuel supply do give cause for concern: (1) localised deforestation, due to regional imbalances between woodfuel supply and demand; and (2) agricultural land clearing (especially due to 'shifting cultivation' and the encouragement of smallholder and commercial farming), which is depleting wood resources more rapidly than energy demand.

In a base case woodfuel demand forecast from 1986 through 2006 by the Department of Energy (Dept. of Energy et al., 1988) it is shown that if no change is made in cooking equipment or techniques, and household woodfuel consumption grows at the same rate as urban/rural household formation, then national woodfuel consumption will more than double (reaching more than 28 million cubic metres) by 2006, unless steps are taken to moderate demand growth. The result will be widespread net deforestation by the early 1990s.

This forecast gives rise to several policy issues with respect to household energy which can be independently investigated to ascertain their feasibility and viability. One issue is whether woodfuel substitutes, such as electricity, coal or kerosene, can be supplied at a lower economic cost than woodfuel. If so, the derivative issue is whether they can be made available at prices which are both affordable to households and sufficient to cover their cost of supply.

Coal as a substitute household fuel

Zambia has substantial coal reserves. Conservative estimates give a total of 13 million tonnes of proven open pit reserves of saleable coal, sufficient for 25 years at present production rates of around 650,000 tonnes per annum. The bulk of these reserves are mined exclusively for the copper mines and a few other industries. It is therefore feasible that the forecast rate of deforestation could be slowed down or even halted if coal is considered as a possible alternative household fuel substitute. Japanese and German studies have demonstrated the technical viability of producing coal briquettes from the reject fines and other locally available ingredients for household energy use.

The major questions arising from the domestic use of coal are distribution, handling and price to the consumer. Introduction of this fuel would also require prior consumer acceptability testing to determine the sociological, economic and environmental (vegetation and landscape recovery and pollution) implications of such a switch.

This study attempts to establish, on the basis of comparative price, the economic viability of the substitution of coal for woodfuel and charcoal in the (peri-urban) areas of severe deforestation. Such a comparison must consider the inter-relationship between various socio-economic and environmental parameters. Since coal prices and demand are invariably affected by the prices of other fuels, it is also necessary to establish cross-price elasticities, the price elasticity of demand and the income elasticity. Both primary and secondary data were collected through visits and intensive literature survey. Most of the information was obtained from government agencies such as the Central Statistics Office, Department of Energy, Forestry Department, National Commission for Development Planning, Maamba Collieries Ltd, Virginia Tobacco Association and the National Energy Council. The work also included desk analysis of the data collected from which an econometric model was made. The model was tested by making several runs on a computer to establish the elasticities.

The market for charcoal and coal

In Zambia, the consumption of charcoal is a predominantly urban phenomenon. Since Zambia is the third most urbanised economy in Africa, after South Africa and Algeria, the policies of government have had the chief aim of keeping the cost of living in urban areas low. This has implied price control on what are considered to be essential consumer items, among which is charcoal. Consequently the price of charcoal has changed very little during the post-Independence era. Of the 50 per cent (approximately 3.5 million) of the population living in urban areas, roughly 90 per cent depend on wood and charcoal for their household energy requirement.

Although coal is mined in significant amounts in Zambia, very little is consumed by households. The price of coal plays a very small role in determining the demand for the commodity. Indeed, the price of coal hardly changed during the 1970s and early 1980s. The only major changes occurred during the 1983 to 1988 period and these were related to currency devaluations.

The model

Since the price of coal does not seem to influence demand, population should play a crucial role. The urban population is crucial in this regard and has been used in the model. Another variable used is the income of the households, which signifies the possibility of switching from 'inferior' energy sources such as charcoal to 'superior' ones such as electricity. The model has used average earnings and has considered a household earning less than 600 kwacha to be poor in Zambia today.

The regression equation thus reads:

$$Y = a + a_1B_1 + a_2B_2 + a_3B_3 + E_t$$

where Y = quantity of charcoal (in tonnes consumed 1975−1986)
  B_1 = the price per unit of charcoal
  B_2 = the urban population, weighted as discussed
  B_3 = per capita GDP
  E_t = error term

A regression of this equation brings the following results:
  $Y = -1126, - 5.7B_1 + 227B_2 + 0.73B_3$
  t values: −1.31 −0.44 2.23 0.55
  $R^2 = 75.5$

Thus only the population parameter is significant at 95 per cent. The model explains only 75.5 per cent of the variance. Dropping the GDP per capita and the price variable does not significantly improve the model fit. However, a log transformation of the equation results in an even better fit. Thus

$$\log Y = 2892 + 57.5 \log X_1 - 596 \log X_2 + 1.425 \log X_3 - 0.13 \log X_4 + 0.349 \log X_5$$

  t values: 2.23 1.44 −2.90 1.56 −0.11 1.64
  $R^2 = 87.5$

where $\log Y$ = quantity of charcoal
  X_1 = price of charcoal
  X_2 = population
  X_3 = per capita GDP

X_4 = price of coal
X_5 = quantity of coal

The population variable, rather than the price of the fuel, plays the most significant role in influencing demand.

Results and policy implications

Since coal and charcoal are sold in different markets, they are considered not to be substitutable at present. However, the potential for using coal as a household fuel exists if due consideration is given to housing structures, cost of appliances, and public education. As the price of charcoal increases relative to that of coal, households may be inclined to switch to coal.

The model indicates that population is the most important factor influencing demand for household energy in Zambia. The influence of population on energy is bound to increase as the population grows and access to electricity and other energy sources remains limited.

The influence of price and income on energy demand may change as a result of the price decontrol policy now under way. In that case, changes in relative prices may be expected to induce increased substitution. For instance, the present uneconomic prices of charcoal may well increase in future, thus inducing a shift to a cheaper fuel such as coal.

What the above suggests is that the switch to coal is a long-term prospect, involving changes in government policy regarding housing structures, pricing policies and income policies. Present housing structures in Zambia, however, are not designed to handle domestic use of coal. Its use would require a shift in design to incorporate chimneys and other draft-creating devices. The shift to coal may also require additional investment in the form of, say, attempts to popularise the use of the commodity. More ominously, even if there were no supply bottlenecks resulting in frequent shortages, would the price remain 'affordable' by the urban population? At present, these are only issues.

Policy recommendations

1. This study and others before it (Dept. of Energy et al., 1988) have shown that the financial competitiveness of electric vis-à-vis traditional charcoal cooking, and the possibility that electricity may also be an economic alternative fuel, suggest that greater emphasis should be placed on the promotion of electricity substitution. This will require an acceleration of the rate of making new connections. Alongside this, it will be necessary to reduce the financial burden of electricity connection and wiring and the cost of the appliances, by using less expensive equipment and/or by spreading the cost over a longer period.

2. With regard to coal, the only feasibility for domestic use is in briquette form. This, however, still requires further investigation into the feasibility of commercial-scale briquette production to determine whether briquettes are viable as a substitute fuel. It must be noted here that production of briquettes may not require any large-scale investments in equipment.

A successful substitution of coal for wood and charcoal must be based on information with regard to the technological and socio-economic requirements as well as the environmental impact of the switch. Further research is therefore needed in these areas before one can even begin to think of substitution.

References

Department of Energy, Ministry of Power, Transport and Communications and the UNDP—World Bank Energy Sector Management Assistance Programme, Draft Report, March 1988.

Food and Agricultural Organisation (FAO), Wood Energy Consumption and Resource Survey, November 1986 (FO: DP/ZAM/E08, Document No. 2).

6 Oil and Natural Gas

6.1 Exploring the Possibility of Using Low-grade Ethanol as a Kerosene Substitute for Cooking

J. Baguant
(in collaboration with R.P. Beeharry and
J. Manrakhan)

The island of Mauritius, with a land area of approximately 2,000 square kilometres, has a population of slightly above one million. Currently the total annual consumption of primary energy, excluding energy consumption for the manufacture of sugar, is around 16 million gj.

With limited hydro-power sites and no proven fossil energy reserves, Mauritius depends heavily on imported refined products — fuel oil, diesel, kerosene, gasoline, LPG, and coal — to meet its energy requirements. For example, in 1987 imported energy represented 65 per cent of the total consumption. The remaining 35 per cent was obtained from hydro-power stations (6 per cent), excess bagasse electricity from sugar industries (10 per cent) and woody biomass (19 per cent). Imported energy represents around 10 to 15 per cent of total export earnings.

Analysis carried out at the University of Mauritius in order to investigate primary energy consumption by end use has revealed that 4,984,000 gj were consumed in 1987 solely for cooking. This cooking energy represented around 31 per cent of the total primary energy consumption for 1987.

On a primary energy basis, kerosene supplies up to 20 per cent (952,000 gj) of the cooking energy requirements. The total cost for its import is around Rs 90 million (US$7 million) for 26×10^6 litres, which represents around 10 per cent of the total energy import bill. It is important to add that there is no government tax on kerosene used for cooking.

Within the general strategy of lessening the island's dependency on imported products through better utilisation of local resources, University of Mauritius researchers have identified low-grade ethanol produced from molasses as a substitute for kerosene. This has been labelled the 'ethanol/kerosene strategy'. The outcome of this exploratory work is presented here.

About 175,000 tonnes of molasses, a suitable raw material for ethanol production, are produced annually by the sugar industry in Mauritius. Some 30,000 tonnes of molasses are used for producing ethanol for various purposes such as rum, vinegar, perfumes, etc. The balance (145,000 tonnes) is exported.

If the ethanol/kerosene strategy proves to be technically and economically feasible, the molasses currently exported could be made available for producing low-grade ethanol for either totally or partially substituting the 26 million litres of kerosene imported solely for cooking.

To investigate the technical feasibility of the strategy, alcohol stoves of the 'Jobo' type purchased from Sweden have been tested using low-grade ethanol. The results have shown that though the flame temperature is comparable to kerosene stoves (approximately 800°C), the power output of the ethanol stove is only 55 per cent (955 w) of that of the kerosene stove (1,750 w).

The ethanol stove has a higher efficiency (50 per cent) compared to the efficiency of the kerosene stove (40 per cent). Stoves working basically on the same principle as those purchased were constructed with locally available material. The modified version has a larger area for combustion and a power output boosted to 1,300 w (around 75 per cent of the power of the kerosene stove).

Taking into account the calorific values of kerosene (36.2 mj/l) and low-grade ethanol (17.8 mj/l), and the efficiency of the stoves (40 per cent and 50 per cent respectively), it has been computed that 1.4 litres of ethanol at 85° purity is equivalent to 1 litre of kerosene. Given the current cost of low-grade ethanol (Rs 3.00/l) and kerosene (Rs 3.95/l), it can be concluded that the cost of cooking with kerosene would be marginally less.

However, the cost analysis is based on a molasses price at Rs 450/tonne, a price which could well be lowered if a national strategy for kerosene substitution is worked out. The ethanol price would also depend on how the plant installation was financed.

When all such factors are taken into consideration, it appears that the ethanol/kerosene strategy is viable and needs further appraisal.

Evaluation of the ethanol/kerosene strategy

Molasses production and consumption

The total annual output of final molasses can vary considerably depending on the total sugar cane production. However, in a normal year with a total cane production of around 5.8 million tonnes and a yield of 30 kg molasses per tonne cane, the total output of molasses can be expected to be about 175,000 tonnes.

Currently some 30,000 tonnes of the total output (17 per cent) are consumed locally and the balance (145,000 tonnes) is exported to Europe and the USA. The quality of molasses is expressed in terms of percentage by weight of fermentable sugars present (i.e., sucrose and reducing sugars). The average fermentable content in the Mauritian molasses is around 48 per cent.

Ethanol production from molasses

Using sucrose conversion equations, and assuming that the Mauritian molasses at 85° Brix contains 48 per cent fermentable sugars by weight, pure ethanol yield could be of the order of 300 litres per tonne molasses.

However, based on our own experience and after discussion with various local producers, a yield of 280 litres of ethanol at 85° per tonne molasses has been used through the analysis.

The cost of producing low-grade (85 per cent) ethanol is computed on the basis of a plant producing 60,000 litres of ethanol per day and operating for 300 days a year.

- The capital investment is estimated to be Rs 84 million (US$6 million) for the low grade.
- The capital would be entirely borrowed at an interest rate of 6 per cent per annum (rate used for developmental projects on Mauritius).
- The lifetime of the plant and repayment period of the loan are 20 years.
- The payment arrangement is based on a fixed annual rate, but the proportion of principal interest changes with each payment.
- Amortisation is based on a modified straight line basis, as implied by the levelised payment formula, with zero residual value.
- Return on investment has been estimated at 5 per cent per annum.
- Raw material cost for molasses has been taken to be Rs 450 per tonne. It is important to add that the price of molasses on the open market fluctuates considerably; however, based on our study, it can be safely assumed that Rs 450 per tonne would be acceptable to the producers.
- Based on the argument given above, yield of ethanol has been taken to be 280 litres per tonne of molasses for low-grade ethanol (85°).
- Thus the low-grade ethanol plant would require around 75,000 tonnes of molasses annually for an annual output of 18×10^6 litres.

The cost of the low-grade ethanol is then computed to be Rs 3/litre. Based on the fact that 145,000 tonnes of molasses are available annually (as shown in the previous section), a total of 40 million litres of low-grade ethanol could be produced.

Use of ethanol as a cooking fuel

In order to investigate the possibility of substituting kerosene by ethanol as a cooking fuel, ethanol stoves were purchased and stove performance tests were carried out to determine and compare their performance relative to other stoves.

Table 1
Performance of stove

Stoves	Flame temp. °C	Efficiency (per cent)	Time for 2l H_2O to reach B.P. (mins)	Power (w)
Electric	—	73	11	1500
LPG	860	49	7	3500
Kerosene	770	40	16	1750
Jobo stove I	820	66	25	500
Jobo stove II	811	50	24	955
Modified stove	820	53	15	1300

The ethanol/kerosene strategy

Based on the results of the stove performance tests, it is found that 1.4 litres of low-grade ethanol (at 85°) is equivalent to 1 litre of kerosene. This equivalence takes into account the efficiency of both types of stoves, i.e. the kerosene stove and the locally designed ethanol stove, as well as the calorific value of both fuels (ethanol 85° — 17.83 mj/l; kerosene — 36.2 mj/l).

Using the above result it can be computed that some 36×10^6 litres of ethanol would be required to substitute all the imported kerosene (26×10^6 litres). This quantity of ethanol would require around 129,000 tonnes of molasses annually which is locally available and is currently being exported. Though the price of molasses fluctuates considerably, it can be assumed that currently, with an export price of Rs 450 per tonne excluding freight etc., this represents an export earning of around Rs 58 million (US$4 million).

If 129,000 tonne of molasses are converted to low-grade ethanol and all the imported kerosene is substituted this would represent a net saving of around Rs 32 million (US$2.3 million) in foreign exchange. However, this net foreign exchange saving would depend on how the project was funded, i.e. from local funds or overseas loans. This aspect needs further investigation.

Table 2 below summarises the relative daily cost of cooking using electricity, LPG, kerosene and ethanol.

Table 2
Daily cost of cooking

Cooking stove	Fuel[1] required/day	Unit cost (Rs)	Daily cost (Rs)
Electric	5.00 kwh	1.75 /kwh	8.75
LPG	0.5 kg	10.01 /kg	5.00
Kerosene	0.95 l	3.95 /l	3.75
Ethanol stove III[2]	1.3 l	3.00 /l	4.00

1. If only one fuel is used for cooking for an average family of 5 members in Mauritius.
2. Refers to stove constructed locally.

Ethanol is around 6 to 7 per cent more expensive to the individual customer as a cooking fuel than kerosene. However, since the cost of producing low-grade ethanol is very sensitive to the cost of the raw material molasses (e.g. a decrease of 10 per cent in the cost of molasses lowers the cost of ethanol by around 6 per cent), it could be recommended that policies be formulated in order to keep the price of molasses used to produce low-grade alcohol at a lower level. A sort of a subsidy could be worked out in order to encourage the ethanol producers and users. This aspect is best dealt with by policy-makers, who have as one of their aims the better utilisation of local resources in the move towards self-sufficiency.

Conclusions and recommendations

Modified ethanol stoves from our laboratories have operated satisfactorily. However, the design could be improved to increase both its power output and its efficiency. The possibility of using other types of ethanol stoves, such as those working on the principle of pressurised fuel where the ethanol is atomised before combustion, should also be investigated. Some work along these lines has already been initiated within the overall energy research programme at the university. Further investigation would be necessary in order to finalise a safe and low-cost design of the device. Parameters like size, weight, construction material and aesthetic appearance need further consideration.

The question of policy formulation in order to stabilise the price of molasses and hence that of ethanol to encourage producers and users, needs further appraisal in the context of long-term planning for optimal utilisation of local resources.

The possibility of increasing the yield of ethanol per tonne of molasses, which would eventually increase the cost of raw material per unit cost of product, has to be further investigated.

For every litre of ethanol produced some 14 to 16 litres of vinasse (distillate slop) is also produced, and for an output of 36×10^6 litres of ethanol around 500×10^6 litres of vinasse would be produced. This waste product, if not properly disposed of or used as raw material for other processes, could become a nuisance. It is of utmost importance that pollution of our environment be avoided. Use of vinasse as a raw material for biogas production has been looked into, but the results have not been encouraging in our context. Using vinasse as a fertiliser, or drying the vinasse to a certain extent and using the concentrated output as a furnace fuel, are other possibilities that need attention.

Only the possibility of substituting kerosene, which supplies almost 20 per cent of the primary energy used for cooking, has been discussed so far. The possibility of either partially or totally substituting ethanol for firewood, which supplies around 60 per cent of the cooking energy needs, could be another option of considerable value in protecting forests, a need which has been emphasised time and again.

Extension work in order to investigate the social acceptance of ethanol stoves operating on low-grade ethanol has to be carried out. Currently this work is also being planned.

An integrated infrastructure for raw material purchase, ethanol production and ethanol distribution needs further consideration.

6.2 Technical Skill Acquisition in the Tanzanian Oil Sector

M.J. Mwandosya

The oil sector is strategic in any nation's endeavour for development. Disruption of oil supplies leads to a disruption in all sectors of the economy. In addition, by holding a prerogative over technical knowledge, the multinational oil companies have strengthened their influence. They have over time invested in research and development in exploration and refining, and have established a world-wide network of marketing systems. A discussion of skill acquisition by indigenous people is a discussion of the interface between the affiliates of these multinational companies, their corporate desires, and the efforts of emerging nations to control or at least monitor and regulate these affiliates.

Skills in science and technology

Developing countries aspire to self-sufficiency in technical manpower. In the case of Tanzania, technical skill acquisition has to be seen in the context of the nation's desire to create a scientific and technological base for development. This desire has been spelt out in the objectives of the national scientific and technological policy, which relate to building up the national scientific and technological capacity, promoting the rational use of resources and encouraging technical innovation. The acquisition of technical skills in Tanzania's oil sector has therefore to be seen as an effort to achieve the objectives of this much wider perspective.

Institutional sectoral responsibilities — an overview

The government's primary objective in the energy sector is to ensure that sufficient energy is made available to consumers in all sectors in a manner consistent with its national social and economic development goals.

The Ministry of Energy and Minerals is the institution responsible for overseeing and guiding the development of the energy sector in order to meet these goals. In discharging this responsibility, the ministry's first task is to monitor, assess, and analyse developments in all the sub-sectors of the energy sector. The second task is to co-ordinate energy-related activities and advise the government on appropriate policy steps to further promote the development of the sector towards the established goals.

The functions of the ministry and each energy sub-sector are mainly focused on overcoming obstacles which stand in the way of achieving the government's objectives in the sector. These obstacles are all generally related to efforts to tackle the two major energy problems faced by both the commercial and non-commercial economic sectors in the country: the high cost of petroleum imports on the one hand, and the high rate of deforestation on the other.

The oil sector

Tanzanian Petroleum Development Corporation (TPDC), a wholly-owned government parastatal under the Ministry of Energy and Minerals, was established in 1969 as the implementing arm of government on matters related to the development of the oil sector in the country. Its mandate is contained in the TPDC Establishing Order of 1969 whereby it is stipulated that TPDC's objectives shall include among others (1) to promote the development of the petroleum industry and the production of petroleum; and (2) to carry on the business of prospectors, producers, refiners, storers, suppliers and distributors of petroleum.

There are five major companies operating oil marketing activities. These are the Tanzanian affiliates of BP, AGIP, ESSO, CALTEX and TOTAL. In the case of BP and AGIP, the government has acquired a 50 per cent stake through TPDC, making them (legally at least) parastatal organisations. However, when it comes to corporate policies and outlook these two oil companies are effectively under the control of their offshore principals. ESSO, CALTEX and TOTAL are wholly owned subsidiaries of their offshore principals. TPDC has a mandate to import oil. Distribution and marketing is left in the hands of these other oil companies.

Four other downstream companies are on the scene on a much smaller scale. Bulk Oil is a locally owned private company. It is involved in transit freight of petroleum products to Rwanda, Burundi and Malawi. To facilitate this activity, Bulk Oil has built a storage depot at Isaka, on the central line of the Tanzanian Railway Corporation. This station, with the assistance of the European Economic Community, is fast becoming an important transit terminal for goods en route to and from Rwanda and Burundi. Bulk Oil is also constructing a depot in Dar es Salaam. Mobil's activities are confined mainly to transit trade. They own some storage facilities at Kigoma, a port on Lake Tanganyika. Shell were part of Shell/BP until corporate reorganisation some years back when all Shell shares in Shell/BP were transferred to BP. Shell are now trying to re-establish a presence in Tanzania, aiming initially at transit business. The Tanzanian and Italian Petroleum Refinery Company (TIPER) was formed in 1963 as a limited liability company. The government of Tanzania, through TPDC, has 50 per cent of the shares while Italy, through ENI's Agip Petrol, owns 50 per cent. It has a processing capacity of 750,000 tons a year.

Employment policies

A policy regarding employment of expatriates is in effect a policy on availability and acquisition of skills. Employment of expatriate staff in Tanzania is governed by the Government Policy on Employment of Non-citizens in Tanzania which was issued as far back as 1966. Immigration regulations of 1986, issued as Government Notice 128 of 1966, stipulate that no non-citizen seeking to work in the country may be granted an entry permit and a work permit unless the Labour Commissioner and the Director of Immigration are satisfied that (1) there is no citizen qualified to fill the vacancy concerned; (2) there is a proper training programme to ensure that a citizen will become available to fill the vacancy by a definite date. Renewal of entry permits of non-citizens already employed is governed by the same conditions. A review of these policy guidelines was made in 1972 with a view to evolving a suitable procedure to make sure that the above guidelines are adhered to. To this effect, parastatal organisations and ministries have set up special committees to look into the question of employment of expatriates in these organisations. These committees' main duty is to advise the minister under whose responsibility the parastatal organisation falls on employment of expatriates, and to ensure that parastatals attain self-sufficiency in trained local personnel. In particular, the committee is required to ensure that (1) no expatriate is granted an employment contract for the first tour of service unless it is absolutely necessary; (2) no expatriate is re-engaged on a further tour of service unless it is absolutely necessary; (3) no expatriate engaged to carry out a special project is allowed to stay after completion of the project.

TPDC, TIPER, BP and AGIP are parastatals, and as such they are guided by the above requirements. ESSO, CALTEX, and TOTAL are privately owned, yet they are also required to conform to the requirements of the 1966 guidelines. The guidelines are useful in assisting the government to monitor the rate of indigenisation and acquisition of skills, and are relevant in that they act as a modifying influence on any corporate plans regarding skill acquisition.

Recruitment policies of downstream oil companies

In order to assess the success or otherwise of the expatriate personnel employment policy stipulated above, in so far as the petroleum sector is concerned, one has to look at the present establishment of key posts. While by and large the implementation of the policy has been successful, contractual obligations require that certain key posts be reserved for expatriate staff seconded from offshore principals. The advantage of this arrangement, in the view of the offshore shareholder, is that it allows the principals to maintain a key role in directing the affairs of the company. To the local establishment, such an arrangement can also be beneficial. It allows the expatriate staff to act as a link between the local establishment and the mother company, facilitating access to technology and the arrangement of training programmes.

The Lubricating Oil Blending Plant began production in 1987. It has a capacity to produce 30,000 mt of various grades of lubricants from imports of base oil and additives. The technology is new to Tanzania's oil industry and the high number of expatriate staff is related to this factor.

In the case of the Tanzanian subsidiary of CALTEX, the offshore principals have only recently (1988) come into a management agreement with a local enterprise, J.V. Trade Services Ltd, for the latter to take over the management of CALTEX. It would seem, therefore, that all oil companies, regardless of their affiliations, have retained control in the direction of companies through retention of the Managing Director's post, and control over finance through the post of Finance Manager. Tanzanians man nearly all the technical, engineering, and supervisory positions.

Training

The oil companies depend on the national school/vocational school system as their main source of qualified manpower. At a national level, however, there is still a deficit in the required number of engineers, technicians and craftsmen.

By and large oil companies do not have a local personnel recruitment problem. Their salaries and fringe benefits are more attractive than those on offer in the public sector. Since basic training at school and college level is not career-specific to that degree, each oil company has its own training programmes. These include in-house training, on-the-job training, field attachment, professional training outside the company and, occasionally, sponsorship to higher institutes of learning. BP, for example, has a well-structured in-house training programme. AGIP has a trainers' training programme which equips supervisors to conduct in-house training for those below them. On-the-job training is carried out, usually by supervisors, in all the marketing companies including the refinery.

TPDC — a case study in acquisition of skills

There are two areas in which acquisition of skills by local personnel is essential for a national oil company whose mandate extends upstream, midstream, and downstream. These areas are negotiations for contracts in marketing, and exploration and production.

Marketing
Although the Establishment Order was promulgated in 1969, nothing seems to have been done to effect its provisions until the second half of 1973.

TPDC's formative years were 1973 to 1977, during which period it concerned itself with monitoring marketing activities, collecting statistics and acquiring knowledge on the working of the oil industry — including the operations of other national oil companies.

During this time Tanzanian personnel managed to acquire knowledge about every aspect of oil procurement. Negotiations were held with various offshore suppliers on selling, purchasing and shipping crude oil. TPDC negotiated crude oil procurement agreements with the Abu Dhabi National Oil Corporation (ADNOC) and the National Iranian Oil Corporation (NIOC) towards the end of 1976, and shipping contracts with the Shipping Corporation of India (SHIPINDIA).

The success of these negotiations, which had taken place without the knowledge of the downstream oil companies, who had until then been the importers of all oil products, was such that from January 1977 TPDC became the sole importer of crude oil.

In order to strengthen its capacity to handle shipping routine, including nomination, loading and discharge of oil, TPDC has drawn on the expertise of SHIPINDIA initially and, more recently, of STATOIL. A marketing adviser has been seconded to TPDC from STATOIL in the context of Norwegian assistance to the Tanzanian petroleum sector.

In all, TPDC's Marketing Directorate has now acquired expertise essential for managing the technical inputs into all negotiations covering procurement, shipping, offloading, refining and sale of oil to downstream. In the case of procurement and shipping, TPDC's technical expertise complements that of other governmental organs such as the National Bank of Commerce, the Bank of Tanzania, the Treasury, the Attorney General's office and the Ministry of Energy and Minerals, all of which are important in facilitating importation of crude and other oil products.

Oil exploration

TPDC's acquisition of skills in the oil exploration field is part of the long-term goal of the country regarding the development of a capability to plan, oversee and ultimately implement exploration projects on its own account. This endeavour has been facilitated by the following factors: the relinquishment of contract areas; international co-operation; and production sharing agreements.

Relinquishment of contract areas: In 1974 AGIP/AMOCO discovered gas in the Songo Songo area. However, AGIP/AMOCO was not interested in developing the gas field, which was subsequently handed over to TPDC for development on its own account. TPDC therefore had to establish an exploration department initially to co-ordinate activities related to the development of the field, and later to explore other prospective areas. The relinquishment of the area provided an impetus to TPDC and the government to recruit and train young Tanzanian graduates in various skills in oil exploration. During on-the-job training, Tanzanians produced a number of studies and reports on the nature and origin of the gas, the extent of the reservoir, interpretation of seismic data, etc. These initial efforts to build a capacity in oil exploration were supported by the Norwegian Petroleum Directorate (NDP) and the Oil and Natural Gas Conservation of India (ONGC).

Since the discovery at Songo Songo TPDC has concentrated on investigating various possibilities for the utilisation of gas. Studies carried out by consultants have provided the corporation with information on gas-utilisation which will prove an asset when projects are implemented. Possibilities range from a fertiliser complex at Kilwa Masoko to the use of gas in industries, transportation, and power generation.

International co-operation: The Norwegian Agency for Development Co-operation (NORAD), through the project TAN 051, has trained TPDC staff in Norway, UK and Canada. NDP's assistance to TPDC also includes joint evaluation of prospects and improvement of its data management system and archives.

Petroleum sharing agreements (PSAs): The contracts entered into with oil exploration companies in Tanzania are in the form of production-sharing agreements. In these arrangements the contractor uses its own resources to explore for oil and recovers costs from the share of production, if and when a discovery of commercial value is made.

Acquisition of skills with regard to petroleum sharing agreements has two distinct aspects. One case concerns the acquisition of negotiating skills in petroleum exploration contracts, and another the implementation of provisions regarding training and use of Tanzanian personnel.

Production sharing agreements follow detailed and prolonged negotiations involving the economics of petroleum exploration and development, legal aspects, national sovereignty, petroleum geology, geochemistry and geophysics, and the transfer of technology. The government and TPDC can now depend on a core of negotiators who have acquired expertise through participating and successfully concluding production sharing agreements.

Sometimes it is necessary to supplement skills with training in more specific areas: a number of Tanzanians have been seconded to offshore consultants such as the Technical Assistance Group (TAG) of the Commonwealth Secretariat. And in areas where specific knowledge has been found to be wanting, especially during negotiations, TAG has provided an expert to be part of the Tanzanian team.

All production sharing agreements entered into between Tanzania and oil exploration companies contain an article on employment and training. This article has been evolved in order to effect 'technical transfer' from the contractor to the local personnel. The contractor undertakes to employ as many Tanzanian citizens with appropriate qualifications as possible, and to set aside an agreed sum of money for this and other training aspects.

Conclusions

I have attempted to highlight the level of acquisition of technical skills in Tanzania. Since this process is part of building up an indigenous capacity in science and technology, the objectives of the national science and technical policy have been reviewed.

The relation of the oil industry to the energy sector, of which it forms a part, has also been presented. The role of the Ministry of Energy and Minerals, and its relation to the parastatal TPDC, have been elaborated, and I have discussed the mandate of TPDC as provided for by its Establishment Order.

The regulations regarding employment of expatriates, though designed to enforce acquisition of skills by nationals, are overridden by contractual obligations such as those requiring that certain posts in the oil industry be filled by personnel from offshore affiliates of marketing companies.

While most oil industry posts are already localised, it should be borne in mind that their tasks involve operation and maintenance. The technologies concerned are protected by copyright and patent laws, and leave no room for innovation or adaptation. For the protection of corporate interests, all the downstream marketing companies have seconded Managing Directors, and in nearly all companies Finance Managers, from off-shore affiliates.

The establishment of a national oil company is one way in which a developing country can dictate the pace of skill acquisition in the oil industry. The role of TPDC in this regard has been highlighted. It is not enough to acquire technical skills. Perhaps more important is the use to which these skills are put. In this regard it will be necessary for a national oil company like TPDC to go beyond mere acquisition of skills and build up a capacity to adopt, adapt, and invent new skills and technologies pertaining to oil sector operation. Research and development should therefore become a priority within such an establishment.

7 Institutions and Planning

7.1 The Effectiveness of Foreign Technical Assistance in Manpower Development in Lesotho's Energy Projects

L. Mohapeloa and M. Lebesa

Evaluation reports and simple observation reveal an abundance of projects which have collapsed. Most projects tend to be supported by foreign aid — technical and financial — and as such have a limited lifetime. The collapse of the project tends to be resource-related — the absence of financial or human resources, or both, to perpetuate the project's activities after the stipulated donor-funded period.

The energy sector as a distinct entity is new in Lesotho, with an institutional presence that goes back no further than 1985. Prior to that, no Department of Energy existed and energy-related projects were hosted by the Ministries of Agriculture, Rural Development, and Water Energy and Mining (itself only instituted in 1978). In strengthening its future programme, the Department of Energy needs to learn the lessons of these previous undertakings.

In addressing the question of manpower development within the context of training and technology transfer, two questions arise:

- What is the goal of the manpower development exercise?
- What is a desirable level of training?

Arising from these two questions is a third: whether the importance of including manpower development as an explicit part of the projects was recognised during the design stage. Further questions and procedures follow:

- What is the intended level of training or technology transfer?
- How does the project implementation schedule accommodate the planned training?
- To complete the manpower development exercise, and in accordance with the above, the trainees must be placed in posts, taking into consideration their training and allowing for further development and promotion during their period of service. The service scheme should include localisation as appropriate.

Approaching this study with the above considerations in view, we gathered information from people who have been involved in the design, implementation and evaluation stages of the project. These included the project financiers — government and a donor agency — as well as project personnel, both local and expatriate.

Methodology

There are thus two principal sources of information for this study:
1. *Government and donor agency personnel* connected with the project, along with the *project personnel*. For this group the method of investigation employed was interviews (where possible) and questionnaires (for the others). Four different questionnaires were designed, to accommodate the different roles played by the government planner, the donor agency, technical assistants and the local project (counterpart) staff. Where interviews were conducted, in general they followed the questionnaires — with, of course, the advantage of re-casting questions to increase the depth of the response. The interviews represent a smaller part of the investigation due to the limited time available to both researchers and interviewees.
2. *Evaluation, mid-term and progress reports* represent another important source of information. A point to be made here is the incredible difficulty encountered in finding these reports. Very few projects have complete reports — a clear weakness in the information storage systems of the ministries. As a result, a lot of time was spent trying to salvage these valuable sources of information. One is tempted to ask whether such reports were ever read, let alone heeded.

There are about nine energy programmes in Lesotho, excluding infrastructure-related energy programmes such as electrification projects financed by NORAD and SIDA and French sources. We appreciate their contributions in the energy sector, though we have excluded them in this exercise. We found that the major focus of these projects was on construction, with fairly limited implications for manpower development. Some analysis had to be made concerning the relevance of the training offered to the locals and the jobs they are engaged in. Are they trained so as to increase the complement of trained manpower in that project, or to take over the positions of their expatriate counterparts, or to achieve some combination of these goals?

We have to examine what the meaning of counterpart training is to the donors. Is it to produce initiators/thinkers or just to produce implementers? At this juncture there should be a clear line of demarcation between training and the transfer of technical knowledge. Is the local who can now comfortably use an electric saw instead of an axe to chop down a tree a trained one? Or should the local have the capability to create what will be appropriately influenced by his resource endowment?

Summary of findings

We have characterised what to us represents an effective manpower development programme. It remains to demonstrate from our findings the extent to which this set of criteria is met, and the inadequacies that become apparent. We have said that the role of manpower development within the national economic development context should primarily satisfy the criteria of self-sustaining development. In this regard there are two principal requirements:

- To create locally the ability to both adopt imported technology and originate technology to suit the local environment.
- To create within the employment structures the appropriate scheme of service, designed to accommodate personnel who have acquired the skills mentioned above.

As regards the second point, it is apparent from both project documents and interviews that in none of the projects was the absorption of staff, and particularly their progression upwards, an issue during the design stage. This is in spite of a signal lack of placements in previous projects — clearly a case of a lesson that has not been learnt. The other and perhaps more substantive issues relate to the method of project design.

- Most projects are designed by the donor agency from its headquarters with at times limited consultations, through a project planning mission. The project planning teams come on two to three week missions and apparently merely to confirm the 'thesis' on which their projects are based. The duration of their mission does not allow adequate time to observe anything contrary to the beliefs they already hold. The input of the Central Planning Office and the implementing ministry is limited. As one official of the Ministry of Agriculture said: 'The donor agencies tend to come to us with a finished product. We need to be protected by our seniors from this type of thing.'

  A rare departure from this type of practice has been the recent extension phase of the Lesotho Energy Master Plan, funded by West Germany and designed in a seminar in September 1987. This type of consultation had the advantage of inputs from all related government agencies as well as the donor agency and its contracted project implementers. USAID and UNDP, on the other hand, have circulated project documents which from all local accounts have had the appearance of a formality. In all fairness to the donor agencies, they make the point that government agencies are lethargic in addressing the questions they do raise.
- We have gained the impression that the government loses the chance to influence the course of projects by not following up effectively. Glaring evidence of this was the difficulty we encountered during our research in finding project documentation and identifying staff who had been involved in the design, monitoring and evaluation stages of these projects. Associated with this difficulty is the matter of high staff turnover, which suggests lack of continuity.

These design problems are attended by two negative effects. Firstly, because the government is not closely involved in the design of the project, it is unable to ensure that it is consistent with the overall drive for self-sustained development. Secondly, and flowing from the first point, the government often overlooks the need to back the project through the simultaneous creation of government posts and an attractive scheme of service. The obvious point is that if the Ministry of Public Service is not sensitized during the design stage, for whatever reason, the problem of difficulty with placements will continue.

Conclusions and recommendations

It is widely known and to some extent accepted that projects financed from outside Lesotho do not perform to expectations. A quick look at their evaluation reports reveals that these projects collapse because there is no local manpower to ensure their continuity.

The question one then asks is: Why can't the locals run these programmes without the guidance of expatriates? This study revolved around that question — is effective technical assistance available for manpower development in energy projects in Lesotho? Our findings have revealed a number of pertinent issues which may have been neglected or just brushed aside. These issues are more or less of a policy nature. Carefully handled, they may help to resolve the problems in the administration of projects after the pull-out of foreign expertise.

One of the most important lessons that emerge from the study is that before the implementation of any energy project, policy level decisions should be made regarding training (the appropriate level) and placements after training. Clear policy on training should guide the formulation of such a project, taking into account all the inputs that are needed and the desired outputs over time.

The training policy should guide on the number of people to be absorbed — manpower needs and necessary skills. This will assist in the recruitment and training of suitable candidates. One of the other major problems that contribute to the failure of such projects is the actual planning of the projects. In most cases projects start off with 100 per cent foreign expertise, and only then begins the drive to recruit locals for further training. It might be beneficial to start with the recruitment of locals and initiate long-term training as appropriate before the implementation of the project.

Trained staff, few as they may be, do not stay with projects for any comfortable length of time for a number of reasons, chief of which turns out to be remuneration. It looks necessary, therefore, for government to address seriously the question of schemes of service generally and remuneration in particular, in order to improve its ability both to recruit and to retain able personnel. The concern is that locals, in most cases, are not trained for and appointed to positions that involve them in decision-making. The planning process of the projects tends to happen without the locals. This concern is raised in the draft report on the review/evaluation of Renewable Energy Projects in Lesotho of February 1988. In this report, it was revealed that 'in most renewable energy projects . . . the implementing staff is always middle qualified technicians and labourers who just do the day-to-day work . . . they are never kept informed about the projects. . . .' And it is further mentioned that 'local counterparts are left out in the planning of activities' they are expected to undertake.

Against the background of all that we have found and observed, it seems to us fair to make the following recommendations:

1. That government should be involved at the planning stage of all projects, represented by the Ministry of Planning, the technical/implementing ministry, and the Ministries of Finance and Public Service. The intention here is to secure at an early stage the commitment of these government agencies so as to ensure their support during the implementation phase.
2. The training activities should be spelled out clearly during the planning stage and incorporated in the project document: the role of trainers, the duration and level of training, etc. The emphasis would be on definite commitments rather than 'appeasing' statements such as 'Training is an important part of the project.' Under such conditions, we would then have training reports to be examined periodically and to act as a monitoring tool.
3. The government and donor agencies should start implementation with long-term training where it is called for, with actual project work commencing upon the return of the trainees. This should permit a hand-over of responsibilities to equipped candidates.
4. All projects should only be implemented after counterparts have been built into the service establishment list, i.e. there should be no problem with the placement of such personnel during the project implementation phase.
5. A system of bonding personnel who have benefited from training under a project should be designed.
6. In order that such bonding should not assume a negative character, an appropriate scheme should accommodate upward mobility of the candidates, taking into consideration their training.

It cannot be denied that the above recommendations represent a somewhat radical departure from the standard. Certainly the new approach could lead to delays in project implementation and, perhaps, a reduction in implementable projects. The important consideration here is, however, whether more projects will be designed and implemented in a fashion that is aimed to serve the long-term interests of the economy, with the specific question of creating local capability being addressed.

7.2 Energy Models as Policy Tools

Joel Morgan

The attraction of models for policy-makers and planners is that they can speed up any decision concerning options in the energy sector. They do this by presenting the energy planner with a set of feasible options between which he can then choose — subject, of course, to the constraints under which he is placed. Models are useful in making any assumptions explicit and providing a required consistency.

Models provide quantitative indications of possible future problem areas in a country's energy system, and good indications of areas that currently require policy intervention. Models can indicate the implications of alternative policies in energy development. In the context of general economic and social development, models can thus serve as aids for planners attempting to ensure that their country's future energy resources can sustain long-term economic and social development strategies and goals. The fact that models depend upon adequate and specific input data may in itself prove beneficial as a result of the impetus created to identify and collect as much relevant information as is practical.

Energy models can help analysts develop pictures of the energy supply and demand balances, energy import requirements, land use impacts and energy plant capacity needs that could be expected to evolve under alternative policy frameworks. A number of technology and policy variables may be explored in constructing long-term energy scenarios. These include cost and benefits, foreign exchange impacts, supply and demand adjustments and alternative energy investments.

The use of computer energy models allows considerable freedom in the specification of long-range energy scenarios, the detailed consumption pattern, the linkages to primary energy sources, demographic and economic growth projections, electric generation system characteristics, petroleum supply assumptions, land use, wood availability, etc. In addition a computerised energy modelling system can be of great use in policy formulation. It can serve as an information bank and guide to data synthesis and development; it can provide long-term supply and demand projections and configurations; and it can compute the impacts of user-selected policy and technology initiatives with respect to the supply and demand balance, capital requirements, costs, benefits, and foreign exchange implications.

Types of models

Accounting framework type models

General features: This type of model has two main functions. It can produce reports on energy balances for historical data and answers the need for data management. It is in fact a core tool for resource assessment studies and can thus answer the question: 'What is the current situation in terms of energy supply and demand?' Desirable features of this type of model would include (1) an ability to accept data in a disaggregated form and to produce reports by aggregating, if necessary, across any category such as by fuel type, household size, income groups etc.; and (2) a capacity to handle the conversion of energy units in a flexible manner, with both the choice of units and the conversion factors being under the control of the user.

Data management features: Accounting framework models are structured in such a way that they are able to handle both aggregated and disaggregated energy data. An energy study usually generates a large volume of disaggregated data and these models fulfil the essential functions of data management which include information access, data sorting, data processing and report production. This is usually done by organising the data into a data base, allowing the various functions to be performed efficiently. Supply and demand data are organised within the following typical structure: (1) by fuel type; (2) spatially; (3) by sector, sub-sector and activity.

The primary and secondary energy flows within the sectors of the economy as well as energy balances are the usual principal data outputs when this type of model is used.

Data processing features: The accounting framework models are limited, by their structure, to descriptive statistical analysis and data cross tabulation. Typical data processing outputs include: (1) the energy supply by fuel type; (2) the fuel demand by type; (3) the supply/demand balance; (4) the percentage distribution of all fuels by type; and (5) the historical trends of the above.

Limitations: Essentially, accounting framework type models perform data management functions and they are not intended to be used as forecasting or planning tools on their own. What this type of model does is to present information in a structured and organised manner. It does not include dynamic relationships and hence cannot show energy sector changes over time. It cannot therefore be used to examine the impact of different policies or energy investment schemes.

Planning type models
General features: The design and execution of an effective energy plan involves the consideration of many wide-ranging issues such as fuel sources

and prices, environmental and land-use trade-offs, energy demand management, energy conservation and changing economic patterns. A little thought will reveal that the establishment of a 'good' set of energy policies and investment programme requires considerable work in the fields of data collection and modelling. Generally, planning type models serve as (1) tools for long-term supply/demand projections under alternative development scenarios; and (2) a means of identifying and evaluating policy options with respect to the supply/demand balance, capital requirements and foreign exchange costs/benefits.

Planning type models encompass linkages between the supply and demand balance to other variables such as economic, fiscal, environmental, demographic, land use, etc.

Policy analysis: Planning type models enable policy analysis to be effected with the use of scenario analysis and sensitivity analysis. Sensitivity analysis is carried out by varying external factors (e.g. prices, incomes) around their base case to determine their effect on the projections made by the model. Scenario analysis, on the other hand, involves choosing a single consistent set of values and using these values to make an alternative scenario projection. Of course, once the alternative projection has been carried out, further sensitivity analysis may be done around this new scenario. Scenario alternatives could include fuel supply enhancement, energy conversion and distribution technologies, end-use efficiency improvement, and fuel substitutions.

Planning type models facilitate policy analysis by enabling one to assess the impacts of alternative scenarios using different criteria, e.g. cost-benefit analysis, environmental impact analysis, balance of payments effects, etc. The possible policy alternatives that could be evaluated include fiscal policy changes for both energy and non-energy items (e.g. prices, taxes, subsidies, etc.), foreign exchange flows, technological options, efficiency improvement options, fuel switching options, land use changes, renewable sources options, and other policy interventions such as environmental taxes, import restrictions, quota systems, etc.

Planning models may also be used to evaluate and study trade-offs such as the use of crop residue as fuel compared with its use as fodder or in other ways, for example. Perhaps more importantly, planning type models may be used for future supply and demand energy projections.

Reference Energy System models

'Reference Energy System' (RES) is a term applied to a description of the energy sector showing the physical energy flows from the primary supply, through conversion and distribution stages, to demand. RES models may also be described as network models or balance models. A typical set of energy flow stages in an aggregate RES is: primary sources; energy processing/transportation; refining; electricity supply; fuel distribution; sectoral fuel consumption; sectoral energy demand.

The specification of the RES will require that each energy flow is subdivided into the relevant number of activities. For example, electricity supply may consist of an oil plant, a hydro plant and a wave power plant. Each activity has to be assigned a process efficiency and a corresponding set of fuel shares indicating how each fuel flow is met from its supply-side activities.

Once a base year RES has been established, future year projections are made by projecting the energy demand for future years, then recalculating the RES flows for each year projected.

The RES output may be presented as an energy balance table which, on close examination, is seen to be a sub-set of the more general RES case.

In spite of being a flexible tool, the RES has some limitations. It takes no account of costs or capacities of the different flow paths and hence cannot directly assist in determining the best future development strategy of the energy system.

The RES data requirements are as those of the input-output models with the following additions: conversion technologies and efficiencies from primary to secondary energy; supply capacity constraints; substitute process technology and fuels; and system losses.

Linear programming: The Linear Programming (LP) approach overcomes the limitations of the RES models. The RES network is reformulated as a set of linear constraints. The costs of each flow and capacity limits are then added, giving a one-period linear programming model. Capacity expansion of energy supply can be added by replicating the LP equations for future time intervals and adding investment variables to allow the capacity to grow over time. An objective is then set for the model by defining the criterion for choosing the 'best' set of energy flows. This could be, for example, the set of energy flows which minimises the economic costs of supply. The model is then solved for this objective. If a solution exists, the supply and demand will balance.

The main limitations on the use of the LP approach are that all constraints and costs must be linear, and that the 'best' criteria may not always be so obvious, and may be dangerously over-simplified.

Goal programming: This is really an extension of the LP concept, having all its strengths, but attempting to overcome some of its limitations. While the LP model allows for the maximisation or minimisation of one objective function, the GP model allows for multiple objective functions to be maximised or minimised, or for a mix of both. Each objective function has associated with it a set of constraints and the objective functions are limited by ensuring that at least one constraint equation is common between any two constraint sets. This approach has the obvious advantage that one may simultaneously examine several issues and incorporate the feedback effects of one solution set into another.

An example of the maximisation/minimisation of multiple objectives would be the following. Suppose a rural system were to be examined and it was decided to maximise the agricultural economy. The objective functions could then be:

- maximisation of agricultural revenue;
- minimisation of energy costs.

Weights could be assigned to each of the objective functions and the model would be solved for each objective function, viewing the others as constraints. LP/GP data requirements are those of the RES model, plus:

- costs of supply primary energy;
- costs of conversion from primary to secondary energy;
- energy import costs;
- costs of devices utilising primary and secondary energy.

Causal models
General features: Causal models by definition deal with cause and effect relationships between component parts of a system. There is no single objective function nor criterion used to evaluate the output. Instead, the output takes into account several criteria associated with policy-making or project evaluation. There is no one criterion which can be identified as being more important than the other in the criteria set. The policy-maker is thus provided with a range of options on which to base his decision-making process, giving him freedom of choice.

Usually causal models are required to answer one main question but may, by the inclusion of secondary parameters, answer several questions. These models may be used for:

- simulation of real world systems;
- tracking physical flows of energy vectors;
- picking up localised effects at a sub-sectoral level;
- tools for policy evaluation;
- modelling of non-linear interactions;
- simulation of integrated energy systems;
- examination of the effects of energy changes on other sectors of the economy by the inclusion of non-energy parameters;
- sensitivity analysis;
- scenario analysis;
- analysis of behavioural changes within the system.

Conclusions

Energy modelling can address itself to the following specific areas:

Policy issues
1. Fiscal policy: what, for example, should be the pricing structure of a fuel

given shortages in the availability of alternative fuels?
2. Trade policy: at what level, for example, should fuel imports be restricted, given considerations of self-reliance, foreign exchange, etc.?
3. Environmental policy: how to control emission level, for example.
4. Commodity distribution policy: considerations of distribution of scarce commodities within the economy.
5. Technology policy: the technological options that should be encouraged, in view of the constraints placed upon the economy.
6. Resources policy: how best to allocate resources and to encourage their generation and extraction.

Planning issues
1. Supply and demand projections: for given projections and growth rates of exogenous variables, assessing future demand and supply requirements.
2. Planning shortages: expected shortages in future inputs such as energy input, capital input, etc.
3. Planning for uncertainty.
4. Social factors, such as assessing impacts of energy availabilities or demands.
5. Supply enhancement: for example, the trade-off between grid extension costs and benefits (by raising living standards, etc.).
6. Resource allocation: would, for example, the return from investments in a particular energy sector be greater or less than from other energy or non-energy sectors?

Project evaluation issues
1. Technology assessment, such as social cost-benefit analysis of a project technology.
2. Introduction of a technology: the net impacts.
3. Integrated systems: the implementation of combinations of technologies.
4. Dynamics, such as the dynamics of enhanced energy output.
5. Economies of scale, such as the relative advantages of household or community systems.

A country, irrespective of its size, needs to articulate an energy policy based on the careful evaluation of existing and future options and their likely impacts in relation to the country's development objectives. These exercises are usually conducted by committees and the like, but a one-off exercise in energy policy analysis will be of little value in the long term. It is much more useful to develop a comprehensive and stable model which will retain its relevance and credibility over the long term, and to utilise it as a tool and guide for policy generation and subsequent analysis.

7.3 Rationality of Kenyan Energy Demand Management

Patrick M. Nyoike and Benjamin Aggrey Okech

This brief evaluation of the feasibility and constraints of Kenyan energy demand management highlights the following issues:

1. The state of the Kenyan macro-economic framework and institutional network, and their implications for energy policy in general and energy demand management packages in particular.
2. Why Kenya needs energy demand management.
3. Common features of demand management packages.
4. Explicit features of Kenyan energy demand management strategies and initiatives.
5. Restraining factors in contemporary Kenya.
6. Research topics in the area of energy demand management in Kenya.

This study covers only the commercial energy sources. We hope to extend it to the non-commercial energy sector in the future.

Energy demand management and the macro-economic framework

That specific planning and policy should relate consistently to an overall national framework cannot be overemphasised. Because of the pervasive nature of the linkages between the energy sector and the rest of the national economy this requirement becomes much more compelling with regard to specific plans and policies relating to energy. It is thus necessary to develop a perspective of the Kenyan national development framework and its implications for sub-policies.

Kenya has a history of systematic formulation and implementation of development plans and policies which dates back to 1963 when the country gained its independence. National Plan document and policy papers have been supplemented by a number of more specific development policy papers as well as shorter-term and lower-tier implementation plans and guidelines. The viability of Kenyan development is manifested in its satisfactory economic performance. Though undermined by rapid population growth, relative depreciation of the domestic currency, and gradual deterioration in the terms of trade for primary exports, the economy has been able to contain a number of socio-economic adversities.

Institutional networks have also been developed. In the area of energy the Ministry of Energy was instituted in December 1979 to deal with energy policy, development and management issues. However, the sector is still largely dependent on development and technical assistance for the implementation of key projects. Functional and operational overlaps and gaps need to be identified more distinctly and evaluated.

Why Kenya needs energy demand management

The purpose of energy demand management is to reduce energy consumption per unit GDP, to control growth so as to reduce its cost to the economy, and to substitute less costly, indigenous energy sources for more costly imported ones. Energy demand management should be seen as a key instrument for socio-economic development as well as a means of environmental preservation. Thus it is an important energy policy and a planning strategy through which both harmonisation of energy supply with demand as well as synchronisation of the important energy sector with the rest of the economy can be achieved. In Kenya a number of factors justify the need for a sound energy demand management package. The major ones are identified below.

First, is the heavy burden the imported crude oil payment continues to impose on the country's limited foreign exchange resources, and attendant negative effects on the balance of payments. The cost of crude oil procurement has increased from about 7 per cent of net Kenyan export value in the early 1970s to about 40 per cent in the 1980s.

Second, is the lack of broad-based indigenous energy resources. Kenya's economy depends on seven sources of primary commercial energy. These are coal (3.9 per cent), crude oil (83 per cent), ethanol (1 per cent) and electricity (12.1 per cent).[1] Of these sources only ethanol is wholly domestic. The bulk of electricity is generated from domestic hydro and geothermal resources. However, about 10 per cent of the total supply is imported from Uganda's hydro resources under a 50-year agreement which will expire in the year 2005. Coal is imported from Swaziland through Maputo.

Third, is the diversity of commercial energy end-users and uses within the Kenyan economy. By sector the end-users are broadly categorised into five: residential, accounting for 8.3 per cent; commercial, 14.7 per cent; industrial, 31.2 per cent; transportation, 41.8 per cent; and agricultural, 5 per cent. End-uses within these sectors vary. However, whereas some uses may be predominant in one sector or may be sector specific, a number of end-uses cut across the sectors.

Fourth, is the low capacity of the Kenyan industrial sector to improve the use of energy. Two factors underlie this condition: (1) the industrial sector is still dominated by those old energy-inefficient technologies which were adopted when the cost of energy was relatively low; and (2) the low productivity of energy use in the sector is still characterised by a failure to invest in demand management measures.

Fifth, is the potential demand for commercial energy sources which exists in the rural or subsistence economy. Such potential demand can suddenly translate into actual demand as a result of such factors as structural change in the rural sector, demographic change such as migration from the countryside to urban areas, or change in the supply base due to depletion of the traditional wood-based energy.

Finally, energy demand management is seen as one of the vital strategies requiring minimal capital injection for overall macro-economic structural adjustment. It has been argued that due to the 1980—87 world recession the developing countries found themselves in special circumstances: lack of capital for adjustment; an unstable oil market; and uncertain interest and exchange rates. Under these conditions energy demand management becomes one of the most attractive adjustment responses.[2]

Common factors

The commonest energy demand management tools are the following:

1. Energy pricing which is used to mitigate against growth in demand for certain products.
2. Administrative measures such as rationing or supply limitations: these have not been used in Kenya as they are considered cumbersome, inefficient and prone to abuse and corruption.
3. Legislative restrictions such as prohibition of use of action equipment, e.g. private generation and vehicles of more than a certain capacity. In Kenya penalties are imposed for driving above stipulated speed limits and vehicles emitting smoke.
4. Fiscal strategies such as those which impose discriminating taxes on certain fuels and certain kinds of energy-using equipment; differential import tariffs; and regressive tariffs.
5. Mass media, through which the need for conservation is addressed — including the prescription of appropriate measures.

Energy demand management has both long-term and short-term dimensions. Short-term measures seek to reduce use of energy by addressing the existing inefficient and wasteful practices. Major examples of such practices are (1) excessive display lighting; (2) under-capacity use of automobiles; (3) altering of thermostat setting; (4) uncontrolled peak demand.

Long-term measures seek to reduce the growth of energy demand relative to GDP through the following methods: (1) replacement of existing energy equipment with new and more efficient models; (2) modification of buildings and retrofitting of existing equipment so as to enhance efficiency of energy use; (3) changing energy consumption patterns; (4) planning economic development according to availability of certain types of energy.

Kenya: explicit features and initiatives

To date the government of Kenya has not published a white paper on energy policy. The government's position can, however, be deduced from a number of its policies and development planning documents. Such documents include the annual economic survey, national development plans, white papers on economic issues and management policies, and annual budget papers. To some extent, government actions and initiatives may also be indicative of energy policy inclinations. However, at times such actions may be in response to short-term and isolated energy and development issues such as management of the balance of payments.

Since all Kenya's petroleum products are derived from imported crude oil, it has been necessary to introduce policies to control growth in demand in order to minimise the potentially disastrous effects on the balance of payments and the realisation of development goals. One such major policy has been the use of pricing instruments to control demand of certain fuels such as gasolines. Gradual revamping of the country's only crude oil processing plant is also being undertaken in order to increase the recovery of desirable products.

Management initiatives for commercial energy demand have spread in recent years as the government attempts to address itself in a more systematic manner to energy conservation in the industrial sector. Thus, as part of these initiatives, the government has set up industrial management programmes through which the private sector is heavily involved; steering and sector committees to facilitate dissemination of information on efficient and cost-effective production and firing technologies; education and training in industrial and commercial energy conservation; and surveys and audits of energy conservation potential.

Constraints

The government has still to develop an integrated and comprehensive national energy policy which clearly models the linkage between the energy sector and the rest of the economy and articulates the various dimensions of energy demand management. At present it is not uncommon to diffuse energy policy issues within different development plan and policy documents. While pervasive relationships and linkages make it possible to address energy issues through macro-economic policies, it is now agreed that such an approach cannot adequately address itself to issues such as demand management.[3]

Finally, we have identified a number of parameters whose constraining implications for industrial conservation initiatives need to be identified and appraised. The study identified thirty such parameters.[4] Nine of them are in the category relevant only to the short-term conservation initiatives. The remaining twenty-one are relevant to long-term initiatives. More generally, they derive from the following:

1. Institutional and organisational structures and capabilities.
2. Process technologies and production hardware engineering technologies.
3. National and energy policies.

4. Criteria and principles underlying the position of industrial investment in innovative undertakings.
5. General management's attitudes and practices regarding training, recruitment and resource utilisation in the industrial sectors.
6. Characteristics and lending practices, of both domestic and external capital markets, which affect availability of capital for investment in conservation measures.

Research areas

1. Assessment and rationalisation of existing demand management: review of the issues raised in discussion and formulation of a suitable energy demand model for Kenya.
2. Evaluation of existing institutional management and recommendation of changes.
3. Assessment of political interests which would affect functioning of the model.
4. End-use responses to a demand-oriented approach, taking into account socio-economic factors, technological mix, financial implications, traditional values, government policies on economic growth, industrialisation, rural–urban migration, employment creation, etc.
5. Identification and appraisal of demand management constraints and the attendant short- to long-term remedies, including options available to achieve these.

Notes

1. See the original unsummarised version of this study for more details.
2. According to P. Armand et al., *Socio-Economic and Policy Implications of Energy Price Increases* (Grower Publishing Company, Brookfield USA, 1987).
3. Ibid.
4. See the original study for more details.

7.4 The Applicability of the 'Bangladesh Model' for Energy Demand Forecast in Ethiopia

Mengistu Teferra

The demand forecasting exercise is indisputably an important aspect of energy planning. Demand forecasts for the modern energy sectors are usually available in Ethiopia but they are based by and large on the trend analysis of past demand, with no deliberate linkage made to the macro-economic development indicators. This problem was encountered in Ethiopia in the course of energy planning as part of the first ten-year development plan covering the period 1985 to 1994.

The reference figure given then for the planning exercise was that of the overall GDP growth rate. One of the first tasks in planning the energy supply was the determination of the demand. However, the demand forecasts that were available were those of electricity and petroleum and these forecasts were actually extrapolations of past trends, bearing no relation to the envisaged GDP growth rate. This posed an almost insurmountable planning problem. For lack of better means, the problem was initially approached using average figures of energy intensity/GDP that were available for other developing countries. The demand figures so obtained did serve as bench marks in the subsequent stages of the energy planning task, which involved adjustment of the plan vis-à-vis other macro-economic guidelines, including the task of pruning down the initial plan to meet investment, manpower and construction capacity constraints.

That experience has contributed to interest in the use of energy intensity/GDP figures in demand forecast exercises. Prior knowledge of energy implications of GDP growth rates envisaged for a plan would help policy-makers immensely. For example, they would be less likely to elaborate a plan that would eventually be rejected on account of impossibly high oil import requirements.

The demand forecast model dealt with in the present project was originally developed by R. J. De Lucia et al. for developing countries in general and Bangladesh in particular. Apart from its preoccupation with the GDP/energy interface, its special advantages lie in its simplicity and transparency. The objective of the research exercise is to test the applicability of the demand forecast model in terms of data availability.

Model inputs, available data and getting around data deficiency

The most important inputs driving the model illustrated in Figure 1 are

(a) GDP contribution scenarios for the industrial, transport, trade and service sectors; (b) energy intensity for various economic and social activities; (c) population size and spatial distribution scenarios. The extent of availability of the input data is indicated below.

Available primary data in Ethiopia: GDP figures

GDP (in monetary units)* by industrial origin at 1980/81 constant factor cost is available for Ethiopia for the years 1988 down to 1973 and beyond. The main socio-economic sectors for which the GDP is indicated in official statistics are the agriculture, industry, distribution and service sectors. Industrial activities are disaggregated into mining and quarry, manufacturing, handicrafts and small-scale industry, construction, electricity and water supply. Distribution activities are disaggregated into trade, transport and communications. Further breakdowns are available at the Central Planning Office (ONCCP). Beyond a certain level of resolution, however, the data have to be worked out, compiled or reconstructed from basic information originating in the relevant ministries and agencies or in the Central Statistics Office.

Energy consumption data

Fairly reliable data on energy consumption (in energy units) are available from several reports and most adequately from CESEN reports for the year 1984. Consumption of fuelwood, charcoal, dung and crop residues, electricity and oil products is indicated for the agriculture, industrial, transport and household sectors. It has been possible to compile time-series data for electricity consumption in the household, commercial, industrial and street-lighting consumer categories. Likewise, it has been possible to compile time-series data for petroleum consumption in agriculture, industry, power generation, defence and other governmental activities, construction and transport.

Population figures

The most recent population census for Ethiopia was published in 1985. The report contains population classification in terms of spatial distribution, urban/rural aggregations, age/sex distinctions and, above all, time-wise projections of these scans. The CESEN report has established the demand for traditional energy consumption for various regions and settings of Ethiopia. This was made possible by combining the results of the population census with the results of an extensive survey on energy demand in various regions of Ethiopia in the first half of the 1980s.

Bridging the gap between the available and the desired

Ideally one should have information on energy intensity (energy

---

* In the national statistics the unit of measure of GDP, in millions, is the birr (1 birr = US$0.48).

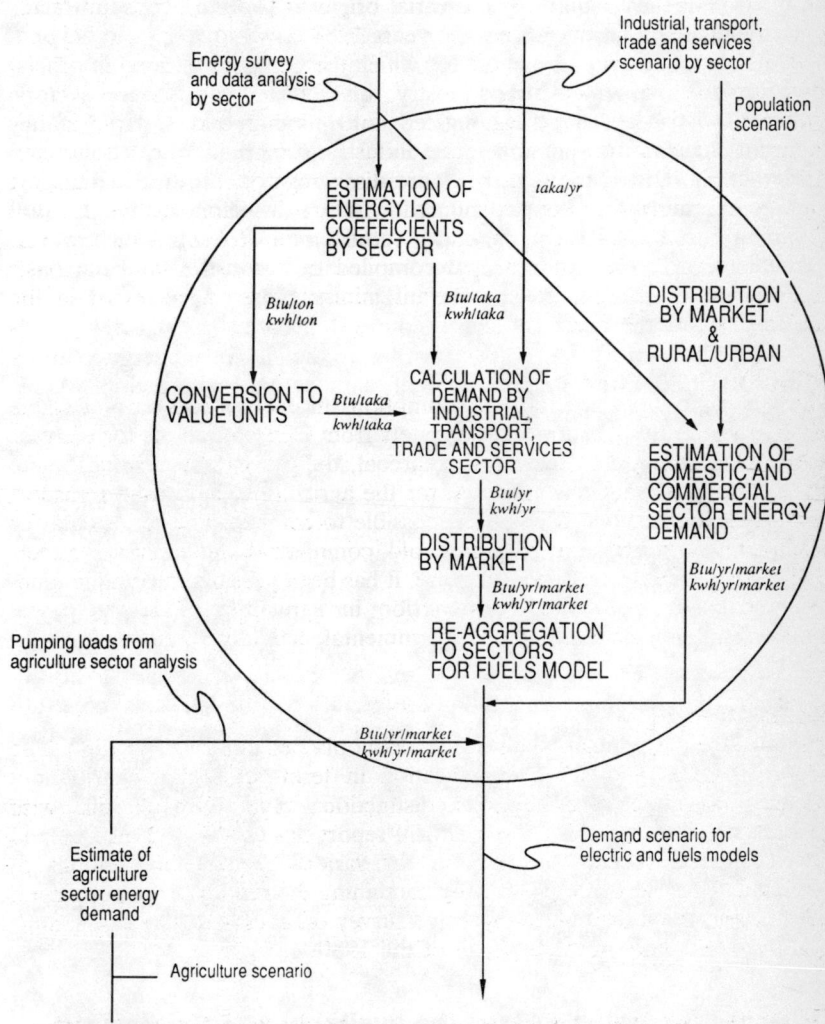

Figure 1. Energy demand data development in the Bangladesh model.

consumption per unit of GDP) on the disaggregate level — e.g., industrial energy intensity figures for textiles, brewery, leather, chemicals, cement, etc.; transport energy intensity figures for land, sea, air transport, etc.; agriculture energy intensity figures for maize, wheat, barley, bananas, etc. Not all these figures are available in Ethiopia, and the data become less trustworthy on the disaggregate level. Furthermore, such data are seldom available for the traditional forms of energy. Therefore the following simplifying approach was adopted.

The modern energy sector

The study of electricity consumption in Ethiopia revealed that industry accounts for about 60 per cent of national consumption. It was postulated that the bulk of industrial electricity consumption went into manufacturing, and so the study focused particularly on this sub-sector. Although GDP figures were available, electrical energy consumption records do not specify manufacturing consumption separately. Instead, statistical bulletins and other publications available from the Ministry of Industry provided the data for establishing the electrical energy intensity per unit of GDP for manufacturing (0.43 kwh/birr). This in turn led to the electrical energy intensity figure of 0.183 kwh/birr for the non-manufacturing sub-sectors. A remarkable degree of conformity was observed between the actual national electrical energy consumption and the consumption estimated using these energy intensity figures along with past GDP data.

A study of the consumption of petroleum energy revealed that, except in the case of fuel oil, more than 50 per cent of the consumption of each product is attributable to the transport sector. In energy terms, about 46 per cent of petroleum energy is consumed in the form of diesel oil in the transport sector. No other petroleum product contributes a similar percentage of energy. It was also observed that diesel oil is mostly consumed in the land transport sector. Having established these basic facts, it was only logical to determine the petroleum energy intensity figure for the land transport subsector. This was found to be 8.38 teracalories per million birr of land transport GDP. A retroactive application of this figure to the transport sector GDP yielded a fairly accurate estimate of the national petroleum energy consumption.

The traditional energy sector

Here the discussion was restricted to biomass-based fuels. The investigation focused on testing the validity of the postulate that the traditional energy demand can be estimated as the product of per capita traditional energy consumption and the envisaged population level. To this end, the 1984 figures for per capita traditional energy consumption in urban and rural settings were used with the corresponding population projections for the year 2005 to obtain a forecast of traditional energy demand in the two settings. The total traditional energy demand for the year 2005 so obtained was less than 10 per cent higher than that predicted by a more complex model.

Conclusion

This research has investigated the applicability of the 'Bangladesh' energy demand forecast model for Ethiopia from the data availability point of view.

GDP data are available for the key energy consuming sectors for the period dating back to 1973 and beyond. National plan guidelines seldom specify sectoral GDP growth rates. However, the problem of distributing an envisaged total GDP growth for a plan period into the different sectors can be tackled using past trends in relative magnitudes of the sectoral GDPs. Such trends may be obtained from regression analysis.

Historic data for electrical energy consumption indicates that the major electricity consumer in Ethiopia is the industrial sector. This fact has led to the need for the derivation of the electrical energy intensity figures in terms of electrical energy consumed per unit of GDP for the manufacturing and non-manufacturing industrial subsectors. National electricity consumption has been estimated for various years on the basis of these figures.

Historical data for petroleum energy consumption indicated that the major petroleum energy consumer in Ethiopia is, predictably, the transport sector and that diesel oil is the major petroleum product used in the transport sector. It has been possible to estimate the national petroleum energy consumption for various years on the basis of petroleum energy intensity per unit of GDP for the land transport sub-sector.

Per capita consumption of biomass energy has been compiled for various regions in Ethiopia in an earlier study. It has been possible to use this data in conjunction with the population census figures to estimate the demand for biomass energy in Ethiopia.

In the case of electricity and petroleum, the actual consumption data closely match the consumption figures estimated using the energy intensity figures referred to above. In the case of traditional fuels, forecasts of future demand obtained by using per capita consumption and population scenarios alone closely match the results established by a more sophisticated model. Thus the available data in Ethiopia permit the use of the 'Bangladesh' energy demand forecast model to derive a first estimate of the energy requirement for a long-term plan. However, the inherent weakness of the forecast model must be kept in mind:

1. Some of the simplifying assumptions are based on the continuity into the future of certain past trends in energy demand.
2. The accuracy of the demand forecast in the Bangladesh model is limited by the accuracy of the GDP forecasts.
3. Inter-fuel substitution arising from a host of causes including fuel availability, fuel price changes, rising standards of living, and major policy changes in rural electrification is not taken into account.
4. Energy demand management and conservation measures are not dealt with in the model.

References

Central Statistical Office, survey of manufacturing industries, *Annual Statistical Bulletin* (Addis Ababa).

CESEN—Ansaldo/Finmeccanica Group, 'Co-operation agreement in the energy sector — executive summary', November 1986.

CSO, *The Demography of Ethiopia: Results of the National Sample Survey* (Addis Ababa, 1974).

De Lucia, R. et al., *Energy Planning for Developing Countries: A Study of Bangladesh* (Johns Hopkins University Press, 1982).

Ethiopian National Energy Committee, *Energy Demand Forecast for the 1976—1985 E.C. 10 Year Development Plan* (Hamle, 1974).

Ministry of Industry, *Annual Statistical Bulletin* (Addis Ababa).

Stanlake, G., *Macroeconomics: An Introduction* (Longman, 1979).

Notes on Contributors

Isse Ali Ahmed is an industrial engineer. He is an Energy Planner in the Ministry of National Planning, Mogadishu, Somalia.

Salim A. Bachou is an economist. He is the Deputy Minister of Energy, Kampala, Uganda.

Jawaharlall Baguant is a chemical engineer. He is an Associate Professor in the School of Industrial Technology, University of Mauritius, Reduit, Mauritius.

M. R. Bhagavan is a physicist and an economist. He is a Research Officer in the Swedish Agency for Research Cooperation with Developing Countries (SAREC), Stockholm, Sweden, where he co-ordinates support for research in the natural sciences, technology, industrialisation and energy.

David B. Brooks is an electrical engineer and an economist. He is the Associate Director of the Environmental Policies Program in the International Development Research Centre (IDRC), Ottawa, Canada.

Ansu Datta is a sociologist and political scientist. He is the Director of the National Institute of Development Research and Documentation (NIR), University of Botswana, Gaborone, Botswana, and is the Principal Co-ordinator of AFREPREN.

Ismail Abdel Rahim Elgizouli is a statistician, with specialist training in operation research. He has postgraduate qualifications in energy management and energy planning, and is a Fellow of the Royal Statistical Society. He is the Deputy Director of the General National Energy Administration, Khartoum, Sudan.

Haile Lul Tebicke is an electrical engineer. He is the Regional Energy Adviser in the United Nations Economic Commission for Africa, Addis Ababa, Ethiopia.

Hailu Gebre Mariam is an electrical engineer. He is the Head of the Major Projects Department in the Ethiopian Electricity Authority, Addis Ababa, Ethiopia.

Stephen Karekezi is a mechanical and industrial engineer, with postgraduate specialisation in industrial management. He is the Executive Secretary of the International Foundation for the Dissemination of Woodstoves, Nairobi, Kenya. He is the AFREPREN Network Facilitator and also edits the AFREPREN Newsletter.

Pierre-Claver Karenzi is a physicist. He is an Associate Professor in the National University of Rwanda, Butare, Rwanda.

Notes on Contributors

Joseph Katihabwa is a physical chemist. He is Professor of Physical Chemistry and Head of the Department of Chemistry in the University of Burundi, Bujumbura, Burundi, where he is also the Director of the Centre de Recherche sur l'Utilisation des Energies Alternatives.

D. L. Kgathi is an economist. He is a Research Fellow at the National Institute of Development Research and Documentation (NIR), University of Botswana, Gaborone, Botswana.

Lucy Mamonei Khalema is an economist. She works in the Lesotho Electricity Corporation, Maseru, Lesotho.

M. S. Lebesa is an economist. She works in the Energy Department of the Ministry of Water, Energy and Mining, Maseru, Lesotho.

Matthew Laban Luhanga is an electrical engineer. He is an Associate Professor in the Department of Electrical Engineering, University of Dar es Salaam, Dar es Salaam, Tanzania.

Ruzvidzo S. Maya is an energy systems analyst with postgraduate specialisation in energy policy analysis. He is the Head of Division for Industry, Science and Technology in the Zimbabwe Institute of Development Studies, Harare, Zimbabwe.

Abel Mbewe is an electronics and telecommunications engineer. He works in the National Energy Council, Lusaka, Zambia.

Dominic Mbewe is an electrical engineer, with postgraduate specialisation in telecommunications. He is the Director of the Department of Energy in the Ministry of Power, Transport and Communications, Lusaka, Zambia.

Mengistu Teferra is an electrical engineer, with postgraduate specialisation in energy studies. He is the Senior Energy Expert and Energy Team Leader in the Office of the National Committee for Central Planning, Addis Ababa, Ethiopia.

M. P. Modisi is a geologist. He is a Research Fellow in the Department of Geology, University of Botswana, Gaborone, Botswana.

Lietsiso Mohapeloa is an economist. He is the Deputy Principal Secretary in the Ministry of Water, Energy and Mining, Maseru, Lesotho.

Joel Morgan is an Energy Planner in the Ministry of National Development, Mahe, Seychelles.

Mark J. Mwandosya is an electrical engineer. He is Professor of Electrical Engineering, University of Dar es Salaam, and Commissioner of Energy and Petroleum Affairs, Ministry of Energy and Minerals, Dar es Salaam, Tanzania.

Alvert Namasamu Ng'andu is a mechanical engineer. He is a Lecturer in the Department of Mechanical Engineering, University of Zambia, Lusaka, Zambia.

Isaie Ntirizoshira is an electrical engineer. He is in charge of electrification projects in the Directorate General of Energy, Ministry of Mines and Energy, Bujumbura, Burundi.

Patrick Mwaura Nyoike is a mathematician and economist, with postgraduate specialisation in energy management and planning. He is the Deputy Chief Economist and Head of Division, Fiscal and Monetary Department, Ministry of Finance, Nairobi, Kenya.

Benjamin Aggrey Okech is a mining engineer and an economist. He is a Research Fellow and Lecturer in the Institute of Development Studies, University of Nairobi, Nairobi, Kenya.

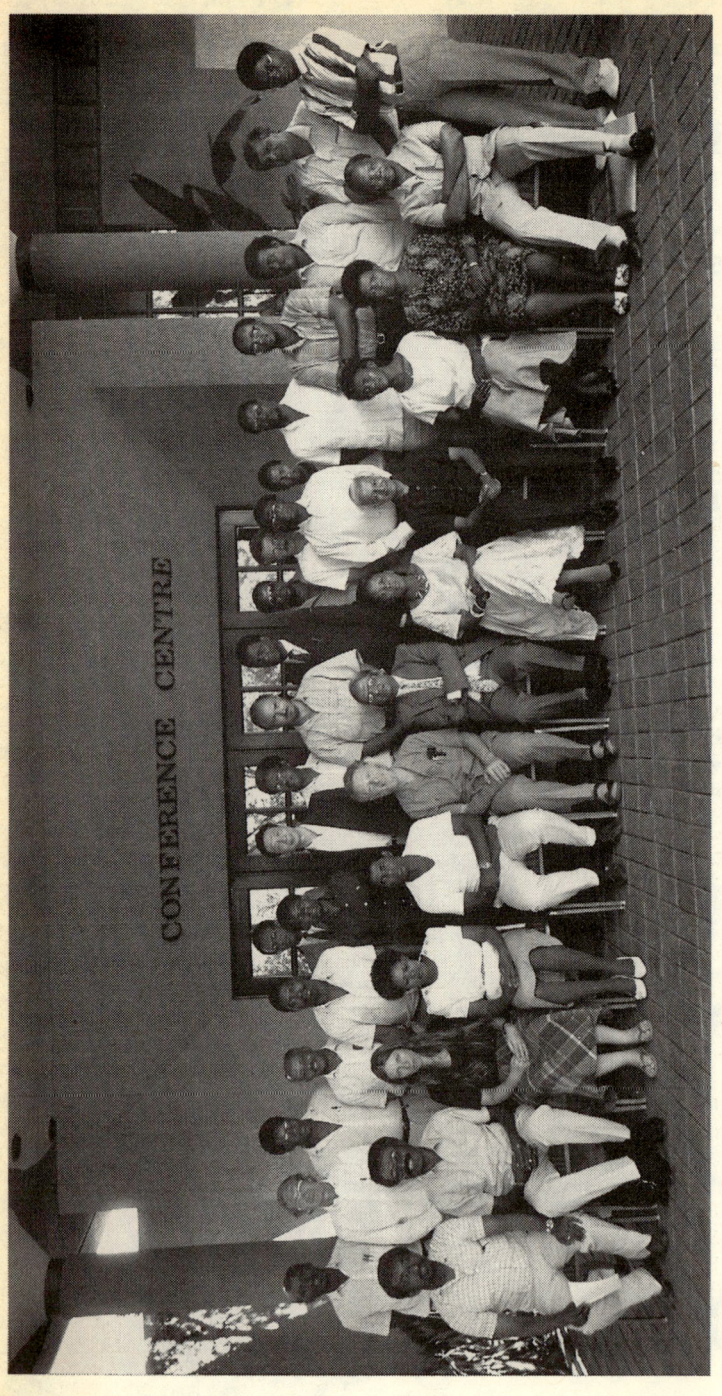

Standing L – R: P.C. Karenzi, D.O. Hall, A. Magama, Haile Lul Tebicke, L. Ntirizonshira, J. Katihabwa, A.N. N'gandu, Mao Yushi, Hailu Gebru Mariam, T. Tietema, D. Mbewe, W.L. Lemo, J. Schroten, P.M. Nyoike, M. Mosimanyana, B.A. Oketch, S. Karakezi, Isse Ali Ahmed, J. Baguant, A. Mbewe. **Seated L – R:** M. Teferra, I.A.R. Elgizouli, T. Turner, G. Raiye, B. Ramasedi, D. Brooks, A. Datta, L. Khalema, M.R. Bhagavan, M. Theko, E. Rakapo, J. Diphaha.

Index

Abu Dhabi National Oil Corporation (ADNOC), 122
aid, foreign, 3, 10, 19, 21, 32, 34, 45, 27—30
Addis Ababa, 58
AFREPREN, xi, xiv, xv, xviii—xx, 3, 45
AGIP, 119—20, 122
Algeria, 107
Amin, Idi, 15
AMOCO, 122
Ampefy hydro station, 20—2
Angola, xix, 57
animal residue as fuel, 5, 16, 38—40, 51—2, 64, 144; see also biogas
Arba Minch, 58—9
Arua District, Uganda, 17
Asia, 57

bagasse electricity, 113
Baidoa, 90
Bangladesh, 11, 143, 145—7
BAT Ltd, 17
Banki turbines, 62
Bank of Tanzania, 122
Berbera, 90—1
bio-energy, xiii—xv, 6, 11; 35—54; see also woodfuel, animal residues, crop residues, etc.
biogas, 16, 17, 19, 33, 43, 44
biomass, 15, 18, 25, 30, 38—9, 41, 48, 113, 146—7
Black Power Ltd, 17
Blue Nile, Sudan, 40
Borama, 90—1
Bossaso, 90
Botswana, xiii, xix, 4, 5, 7, 48—54, 99—105
Botswana Breweries, 103
Botswana Meat Commission, 103, 105
Botswana Renewable Energy Technology Project (BRET), 52
Botswana Power Corp., 100, 102—3
BP, 119—21

BRARUDI (breweries), 27
Bulk Oil, 179
Burua, 90—1
Bujumbura, 26—9, 82
Burundi, xiii, 3, 4, 6, 26, 42, 81—6, 119
Burundi National Bureau of Study Projects (BUNEP), 42

Caltex, 119—21
Canada, 123
CEAER, 43
CESEN, 58
charcoal, 5, 8, 16—7, 27, 30—32, 38—40, 42, 45—6, 106—10, 144
China, xiii, 59
coal, xiii—xiv, xvi, 7—8, 10, 25, 31, 53, 89, 91, 93—110, 139
coal briquettes, 31, 33, 44, 107, 110
Commonwealth Science Council, 17, 31
Commonwealth Secretariat, 123; Technical Assistance Group (TAG), 123
copper, 8
COTEBU textile plant, 86
crop residue as fuel, 5, 16, 38—40, 42, 45, 64, 97, 134, 144; see also ethanol, etc.

Dar es Salaam, 119
deforestation, 1, 5, 31, 37, 39—40, 42, 44, 106—7
dielectric heating, 83—4
diesel, 6, 15, 57—61, 90—93, 113, 147
Direction Générale de L'Energie, Rwanda, 46
Ditshegwane, 52
Djibouti, 89
drought, 6, 37, 50
Dukwe, 50, 52

East Africa, xvii, xix, 57, 64
Ecole Polytechnique Federale de Lausanne (EPFL), 42, 44

education and training, xi, 5, 7, 10, 22, 45, 50, 62, 81, 97, 118, 120—22
electricity, xiii—xv, 6—7, 11, 27, 29, 39, 57—86, 89—93, 99, 108—9, 116, 128, 135, 139, 143—4, 146—7; *see also* bagasse, geothermal, grid extension and hydro power
Electricity Supply Commission of South Africa (ESCOM), 64, 66—7
energy, conservation, 6, 10—11, 18, 68—80, 134, 140—1, 147; costs, xv—xvi, 6—9, 29—30, 67—8, 74—5, 80, 84—6, 92—3, 107—9, 114—6, 136; demand management, 10—11, 134, 138—48; wastage, 70, 73, 77—80
ENEE, 89—90
environmental degradation, xi, 1, 5, 31, 37, 39, 95, 97, 103, 110, 134, 137
Erigavo, 90
ESSO, 119—20
ethanol, 8, 9, 82, 113—17
Ethiopia, xiii, 6, 9, 11, 58—9, 89, 91, 93, 143—48; Central Planning Office, 144; Central Statistics Office, 144; Ministry of Agriculture, 59; Ministry of Industry, 145
Ethiopian Electricity Authority (EELPA), 59
Europe, 114
European Economic Community, 119
Expanded Coal Utilisation Project (ECUP), 102
export earnings, xii, 8—9, 15, 25, 99, 101, 103, 113—4, 116, 141

finance, private sector, xv, 23; government subsidies, xv, 7, 34, 64, 68, 127; *see also* aid, foreign
forestry, 5, 16, 18, 40—1, 44—5, 97, 106, 117; *see also* deforestation
foreign exchange, 57, 61, 65, 71, 76, 81, 132
France, 128
Francistown, 102
fuel imports, xi, 8, 9, 25, 103, 113, 116, 137, 139, 141
fuelwood, *see* woodfuel

Gaborone, xiii, xv, 50, 102, 104

Gakutwe, 53
gases, natural, xiii, xvi, 7, 66, 83, 91, 111—24; Liquified Petroleum Gas (LPG), 27, 116
geothermal energy, 10, 15, 16, 19, 30, 139
Germany, 93, 107, 129
Gezira province, Sudan, 40
Ghana, xiii
Gitega, 82
'glass house effect', 26
Goodhope, 51
grid extension electricity, 57—63, 137

Hargeisa, 90—1
household energy use, 6, 7, 11, 16, 23, 27, 29, 37—41, 50, 52—3, 58, 64, 66, 79, 83, 91, 94—8, 102, 104, 106, 108—9, 137
hydro power, 6, 10, 18—19, 21, 30, 32, 65, 69, 77—8, 80, 86, 89, 90, 106, 113, 135, 139; small-hydro plant, 57—64, 82
hydraulics, 25

India, 9
induction heating, 83
industrial energy use, 7, 8, 17, 24, 27, 50, 61, 104, 123, 141, 144, 147
International Development Research Centre (IDRC), xiii, xix, 46
Isaka, 119
Italy, 119

Japan, 107
Jelib, 90
Jinka, Ethiopia, 58—60
Joint Energy and Environment Projects (JEEP), 17
Juba river, 90
Jurassic Karoo Supergroup, 99
J.V. Trade Services Ltd, 121

Kafue Gorge Power Station, 77—8, 80
Kenya, xiii, 3, 8—9, 20, 138—42
Kenya Ceramic Jiko (KCJ) project, 20—3
kerosene, 8, 40, 106, 113—7
Kgalagadi Breweries, 103

Kgatleng, 51
Khartoum, 38
Khubetsoana, 65, 68
Kigali, 42–3, 46
Kigoma, 119
Kijito wind pump, 20–1
Kilwa Masoko, 123
Kismayo, 90
Kitwe, 31
Kivu lake, 44
Konso, 59
Kweneng, 51–3, 101

Lakas Products Pvt. Ltd, 94
Latin America, 57
Lesotho, xiii, xix, 9, 10, 64–8, 127–31; Central Planning Office, 129; Department of Energy, 127; Development Committees, 68; Housing Corporation, 68; Ministry of Agriculture, 127, 129; Ministries of Rural Development, Water Energy and Mining, 127; Ministries of Planning, Finance and Public Service, 131
Lesotho Electricity Corporation, 6, 66–7
Lesotho Energy Master Plan, 129
lignite, 83
Lobatse, 104
The Lubricating Oil Blending Plant, 121
Lusaka, 78–9

Maamba Collieries Ltd, 33, 107
Mabotle stove programme, 22–3
Madagascar, 20–1
Maki river, 59
Malawi, 119
Mantsonyane, 64
Maputo, 139
Maseru, 6, 64–5
Masunga, 51
Matabelena, 51
Mauritius, 8, 113–5
Mazoe Citrus Estates, 94–6
Mberengwa, 94, 97
methane gas, 44, 82
Mmamabula, 7, 99–101, 103–4
Mogadishu, 7, 89–90
microwave heating, 84
migration, 65–6

mining, 15, 65
Mobil, 119
Morupule, 99–104
Mozambique, xiii
Mugere, 82
Murewa, 94–5, 97

National Bank of Commerce (Tanzania), 122
National Iranian Oil Corporation (NIOC), 122
National University of Rwanda, 5, 43, 46
Neri river, 59–60
Norway, 9, 122–3
Norwegian Agency for Development Co-operation (NORAD), 32, 123, 128
Norwegian Petroleum Directorate (NDP), 123
NIR (University of Botswana), xiii, xix, xx, 46
NGOs, xx, 4, 17–8, 24, 42, 45

oil, xiii, xvi, 7, 9, 64, 69, 70, 82–6, 89, 99, 111–24, 135, 139, 140–1, 144
Oil and Natural Gas Corporation of India (ONGC), 123
Omo river, 59
Oodi, Botswana, 49

peat, 6–7, 25, 82–6
petroleum products, xi, xiv, 7–11, 15–6, 25, 39, 57, 69, 81–2, 106, 113, 119-20, 123, 141, 143, 147; see also oil, diesel, etc.
photovoltaics, 30, 33; see also solar energy
planning for energy, xi–xvii, 9–11, 21, 30, 32, 48, 68, 89, 100, 116, 127, 130, 132–7, 143
pollution, xvi, 7, 83, 94–100, 105, 117, 140
population increase, 5, 42, 106, 109

Qardo, 90

Ramotswa, 104
Reference Energy System (RES), 134–6

156 Index

Renewable Energy Technologies (RETs), xii–xiv, 3–4, 19–30
Renewable Energy Projects, 30, 130; *see also* wind, solar, hydro and biomass energy
research, xi–xvii, 9–10, 22, 24, 30–4, 46, 48–9, 53, 62, 65, 89, 109, 113–8, 124, 128, 132
resistance heating, 83
Rural Industries Innovation Centre, 52
Ruzizi I and II, 82
Rwegwa, 82
Rwanda, xiii, 4–5, 42–7, 83; National Energy Policy, 5, 119

Seoli, lower, 65
Semonkong, 64
Selebi Phikwe Power Station, 50, 102
Seychelles, xiii, xix, 9
Shell, 119
Shipping Corporation of India, 122
Shurugwi, 97
Singida, 70
SIDA, 128
solar energy, 4, 15, 17, 19–22, 25–9, 30, 32–3, 43–4
Songo Songo, 122–3
Somalia, xiii, 7, 89–93
South Africa, 65, 107
Southern Africa, xvii, xix, 3, 46, 57, 64, 99
STATOIL, 122
steam turbines, 91
Sua Pan soda ash project, 103
Sub-Saharan Africa, xi–xiii, 3–4, 20–24
Sudan, xiii, xix, 4, 5, 37–41; National Energy Administration, 5, 38
Swaziland, xiii, 139
Sweden, xiii, 8, 114
Swedish Agency for Research Co-operation with Developing Countries (SAREC), xiii, xv, xix, 45–6
Switzerland, 42, 44–5

Tanganyika, Lake, 27, 119
Tanzania, xiii, 9, 42, 69, 118–24; Attorney General's Office, 122; Ministry of Energy and Minerals, 118–9, 122, 124; Government Policy on Employment of Non-Citizens, 120; Government Notice 128 of 1966, 120; Treasury, 122
Tanzanian Electric Supply Company Ltd (TANESCO), 69–76
The Tanzanian and Italian Petroleum Refinery Company (TIPER), 119–20
Tanzanian Railway Corporation, 119
theft of power, 6, 77–80
thermal power, 27, 57, 68–71, 73–6, 90–1, 93
Third Five Year Development Plan (Lesotho), 65
transport, xiv, 11, 16, 103–4
Tsenola, 65
Tsosane, 65

Uganda, xiii, 3–4, 10, 15–9, 42, 139; Ministry of Energy, 10, 17–18; Ministries of Environment Protection, Power, Transport and Communications, 17
UNEDO, 4, 18–9
United Kingdom, xiii, 20, 123
United States of America, xiii, 114
University of Botswana, xiii, xviii, xix, 4, 50
University of Burundi, 29
University of Mauritius, 113
UNCTAD, xvi
UNDP, 16–7, 45, 129
USAID, 20, 129
Usika Crafts, 17

Virginia Tobacco Association, 107

Wankie Colliery Company, 94–5
wave power, 125
White Nile, Sudan, 40
wind energy, 15, 20–2, 30, 32
woodfuel, xiv, 4–5, 7–8, 15–18, 27, 37–40, 42–3, 48–54, 64, 95–6, 102, 104–6, 110, 117, 132, 144
World Bank, xvii, 17, 45, 85; ESMAP, 19

Yamba, Prof. Francis D., 31–2

Zaire, 42, 82
Zambia, xiii, 3—4, 6, 8, 30—3, 77—80, 106—10; Central Statistics Office, 107; Department of Energy, 32—3, 107; Ministry of Science and Technology, 34; National Energy Council, 107; National Commission for Development Energy, 107; National Council for Scientific Research, 33
Zambia Electricity Supply Corporation Ltd (ZESCO), 77—80
Zimbabwe, xiii, 7, 8, 94—8